SOCIAL CAPITAL IN AMERICA

SOCIAL CAPITAL IN AMERICA

COUNTING BURIED TREASURE

Brian J. Jones

Paradigm Publishers
Boulder • London

Copyright © 2011 Paradigm Publishers

Published in the United States by Paradigm Publishers, 2845 Wilderness Place, Boulder, CO 80301 USA.

Paradigm Publishers is the trade name of Birkenkamp & Company, LLC, Dean Birkenkamp, President and Publisher.

Library of Congress Cataloging-in-Publication Data

Jones, Brian J.
    Social capital in America : counting buried treasure / Brian J. Jones.
        p. cm.
    Includes bibliographical references.
    ISBN 978-1-59451-884-3 (hbk. : alk. paper)
    ISBN 978-1-59451-885-0 (pbk. : alk. paper)
    1. United States—Social conditions—1980-   2. Social capital (Sociology)—United States.   3. Social problems—United States.   I. Title.
    HN59.2.J647 2011
    306.0973—dc22

                                                                            2010046150

Printed and bound in the United States of America on acid-free paper that meets the standards of the American National Standard for Permanence of Paper for Printed Library Materials.

Designed by Straight Creek Bookmakers.

15 14 13 12 11
1 2 3 4 5

To Suzanne:
My shiniest piece of social capital.

Contents

Preface and Acknowledgments   *ix*

1 "What Is *Wrong* with People?"   1

2 Designing a Model of Social Capital   8

3 Work   19

4 Family   29

5 Social Networks   38

6 Voluntary Association   51

7 The Model of Social Capital   68

8 Modeling Trends   84

9 Social Capital and Social Inequality   96

10 Social Capital Futures   107

Notes   *118*

About the Author   *129*

Preface and Acknowledgments

This project all started at a Borders several summers ago.

I had perused the science fiction offerings and was proceeding to the martial arts section, when I found myself at a display case in an area with books for grown-ups. The featured volume was *Bowling Alone* by Robert D. Putnam. Like everyone else, I was intrigued by the title, then impressed by the weighty claims of true heavyweights on the book jacket. But it was when I opened the tome that intellectual lightning struck. Here was a sweeping vision of the real heart of American life in its neighborhoods, homes, schools and, most pointedly, voluntary associations. Moreover, that vision was beclouded not by political cant or media sound-bites, but by real social science data. Putnam actually put factor analysis—a forbidding statistical technique for most—right into the text of a book I was reading in Borders. Breathtaking.

Bowling Alone inspired me to widen and deepen my own vision of American life beyond social networks to the more expansive concept of social capital. Coming to grips with Putnam's analysis of its myriad forms forced me to develop my very own model of *Social Capital in America* consisting of work, family, social networks and voluntary associations. Much of the book is devoted to demonstrating the primacy of these everyday social structures and how they intertwine in our lives. For this, the Social Capital Community Benchmark Survey masterminded by Putnam and his Saguaro Seminar colleagues has been indispensable. *After* the model-building, one can then address trends in American society using the extraordinary cumulative General Social Survey tracking each form of social capital all the way back to 1972.

Since its inception, friends and followers of *Social Capital in America* have prompted me to skip all the numbers and report the news in straightforward verbal summaries. I could not do it. Truly, the data *are* the news. The subtitle is "Counting Buried Treasure" because the stockpile of these precious things goes largely unreported. I report it using tables that are easier to read than a baseball box-score and figures that are backed up by serious statistics, but are also as accessible as a *USA Today* graph.

Nevertheless, a quick flip-through will establish that this is an odd-looking book. Despite its unconventionality, Mick Gusinde-Duffy of Temple University Press has been an advocate of *Social Capital in America* from the very start. When things stalled at Temple, Mick strongly recommended that I seek out Paradigm Publishers, which he characterized as a first-rate operation which would lavish special attention on a small number of high-quality books. I can vouch for the former, and hope that the book in its present form can aspire to the latter. Jason

Barry has been an able and amiable facilitator of every facet of the project. The other Jason, Dr. Potter, was indispensable in creating a finished product out of a very raw manuscript. Based on my previous contacts with large publishing houses, it has been a truly unique experience to deal directly with the president, Dean Birkenkamp, on the nuts-and-bolts of a book.

And finally I must recognize folks in my own shop at Villanova University. Dana Moss, then research associate in the sociology department and now ascending to the professorate, was a ruthless editor and a sympathetic sounding-board. Elisa M. Wiley spent much of this past year learning and implementing the nuances of camera-ready copy to make the book a reality. My debt to both of them is just another manifestation of *Social Capital in America*.

1

"What Is *Wrong* with People?"

> Things fall apart; the center cannot hold;
> Mere anarchy is loosed upon the world...
> —*William Butler Yeats,*
> "The Second Coming"

Many Americans think that American society is falling apart. Some people are terrified of terrorism; lots of people are scared of crime; practically everybody worries about the economy. But the question "What is wrong with people?" bespeaks a whole different kind of concern. It is the ominous sense that most Americans are, well, no damn good. It is less about everyday villains, and more about the villainy of Everyman and Everywoman.

This introductory chapter will chart the looming shadow of societal break-down in public opinion, but first do a reality check on your own life. Do you hear family members mouth a version of the what-is-wrong-with-people question as they channel surf through daytime talk shows? Do you hear the question in their voices as co-workers discuss the latest baby strangulation, priest mole-station or school shooting? Do you yourself sense a rising tide of evil among fellow citizens?

Of course, the fear of things falling apart has haunted America throughout its history. The colonies of 17th century Massachusetts invented the New Eng-land town meeting to involve all in community life, and then worried about its decline when founding idealism gave way to vituperous votes.[1] Every school child knows of the contention among they who would become "Founding Fa-thers" over whether the colonies should even enter the Revolution, and how they should form a society thereafter. In the following century, a famous foreign visi-tor appeared, driven by the ghastly dissolution of his own nation (in the French Revolution) to survey civil society in America; Alexis de Tocqueville's tour of this "nation of joiners" revealed ample anxiety among its citizens about just how securely they were joined together. In the 20th century, the Great Depression gave rise to great concerns about the very foundation of the nation.

Current concerns about societal breakdown have a distinctive character– they are *about* character. The "What is wrong with people?" refrain seems in-creasingly rhetorical. What is *wrong* with Americans seems to be that they do not care enough about other Americans.

1

POLLS

Scientific public opinion polling is too new to track a baseline all the way back through U.S. history, but the fear and loathing levels then could hardly have been higher then than they are now. Many of the polls explicitly introduce the time dimension by asking whether things are getting better or worse.

According to renowned pollster Daniel Yankelovich,

> ...public distress about the state of our social morality has reached nearly universal proportions: 87 percent of the public fear that something is fundamentally wrong with America's moral condition, up from 76 percent a year ago. In general, a widespread feeling of moral decline has sharply expanded within the public in the last two years, regardless of gender, age, race or geographical area.[2]

Gallup replicated these findings with 78 percent of the public calling "the state of moral values in this country" either very or somewhat weak, and with an almost identical percentage saying that that "state" had deteriorated over the past 25 years.[3] Stretching the timeline backward, 67 percent of Chilton Research Services respondents think that "the U.S. is in a long-term moral decline."[4] Personalizing the issue by "thinking back to when you were growing up...," the share of the public responding that "social and moral values" used to be "higher than today" is, again, 67 percent.[5] Clearly, the public perception is that America is losing its collective soul and redemption is not at hand.

Just as clearly, there is a highly suspect source of this moral breakdown—family breakdown. A Public Agenda study which listed its first finding as "The Moral Meltdown" also listed its third finding as "Careless Parents":

> American believe that parents are fundamentally responsible for the disappointing state of today's youth. People say parents fail to teach youngsters right from wrong and to pass on the values children need to learn...[6]

And people link this failure to social breakdown; a Fox News poll in 2000 indicated that no less than 80% of the country see our children's behavior as evidence that we are in a moral crisis.[7]

A striking feature of these public perceptions is their reflection of C. Wright Mills' famous contrast of "personal troubles" versus "public issues."[8] Apparently, many Americans feel that their *own* moral and family lives are just fine, so the breakdowns must be occurring in *other* people's souls. A Pew Research Center poll found only 2 percent of Moms to be dissatisfied with the child-rearing job they are doing. Three out of four adults say that they meet their own social commitments, but 90 percent say that a "major problem with society" is that other people do not.[9] Mills' phrase is often used to separate the sorrows suffered by individuals from the social problems suffered by society. In that vein, a Gallup poll on "the most important problem facing this country today" has shown "ethical/moral/family decline" to crack the top ten—ahead of social problems such as racism, the environment and AIDS.

Even more compelling evidence on the sour public mood about America is available in a Gallup poll series that puts the question this way: "In general, are you satisfied or dissatisfied with the way things are going in the United States at this time?" In every month since January 2004, the majority of Americans polled said they were "dissatisfied" with the society. Remarkably, in May of 2008—before the ravages of the "Great Recession"—this negative opinion reached a full 85%.[10]

BOOKS

To stroll through a contemporary bookstore is to stroll through sin. Autobiographies are stuffed with accounts of personal and family dysfunction; the self-help section offers advice on how to become a "promise keeper" to oneself and others; even the sociology section is stacked with stories of social killers. A growing genre is books devoted to the "What is wrong with people?" question. Consider this partial list of titles,[11] all published since 1996:

Charles Derber, *The Wilding of America: How Greed and Violence Are Eroding Our Nation's Character.*
Frank Hearn, *Moral Order and Social Disorder: The American Search for Civil Society.*
Richard Sennett, *The Corrosion of Character.*
John A. Hall and Charles Lindholm, *Is America Breaking Apart?*
Robert Bork, *Slouching Towards Gomorrah.*

Despite the title of the last (a line from the same Yeats' poem that opened this chapter), these are accounts of much more than sin. There is moral decay, but it is attached to some form of *social* decay—too much selfishness to be concerned about others; too much concern with personal rights and too little concern with family; too much care about commodity to bother with community. In other words, attention is turned from immorality onto the (increasingly pockmarked) face of society itself.

Enter "Bowling Alone," a 1995 essay—and 2000 book of the same title[12]—in which Harvard political scientist Robert D. Putnam transformed the discourse on American decline. Essentially, he upped the magnification from personal breakdowns in marriages, malls or markets to a panoramic view of societal breakdown. The title refers to fact that bowling is up in America but bowling *teams* are down, which Putnam takes to be emblematic of withdrawal from churches, PTA's, voting booths, dinner parties—indeed, from every form of association on which he turns his instruments. Both the sweep of Putnam's subject and the sophistication of his instruments are impressive. In the 2000 book, Putnam marshals three major longitudinal datasets and multivariate statistical analyses to unveil, as his subtitle put it, "The Collapse... of American Community."

But all are not convinced that American society's sky is falling. Everett C. Ladd, past president of the Roper Center for Public Opinion Research, has argued that Putnam is just plain wrong. To support his argument, Ladd imitates Putnam by arraying data in kitchen sink-like fashion to constitute "A Vast Empirical Record [that] Refutes the Idea of Civic Decline."[13] There is some point-counterpoint analysis (Putnam: PTA membership down; Ladd: school-board meeting attendance up), but essentially both cases rest on the considerable weight of pie charts, tables and trend lines supporting decline versus no decline. *Bowling Alone's* status as a bestseller would certainly indicate that Putnam's thesis resonates with the public mood, but the question hangs in the air: Whom should we believe?

CIVIC TASK FORCES

One official signal that a concern has become a consensus social problem is the formation of a blue-ribbon task force. Panels of politicians and pundits have been swarming all over the get-involved-with-the-community issue. The "Council on Civil Society" recently formed "…because we are using up, but not replenishing, the civic and moral resources that make our society possible;"[14] its members include Vice-Presidential candidate Senator Joseph Lieberman, pollster Daniel Yankelovich, and assorted high-profile professors who have commented on American decline. The University of Pennsylvania formed the "Penn National Commission on Society, Culture and Community" to focus on deteriorating public discourse caused in part by "…the Fragmentation of Communities, in which race, class, ideology, ethnicity, and special interests divide and sub-divide rather than unify civic life;"[15] ex-Senator (and Knick) Bill Bradley, and author E. L. Doctorow are among its luminaries.

The profusion of such high-profile panels/commissions/councils is truly extraordinary. A simple Google search using the simple section heading "civic task forces" yields over 2 million hits and a multitude of regional, statewide, community-based and university based organizations. Or consider an internet search for "civic engagement." This once-fuzziest of academic buzzwords now strikes over a million sites. In both the public arena and the public mind, American disengagement and decline appear to be such a foregone conclusion, such an "of course" phenomenon, that now we must seek expert-driven solutions.

SOCIAL CAPITAL

Clearly, Robert Putnam's work has transformed the terms of the debate on the state of America. Piecemeal patterns of social breakdown have given way to global generalizations about societal decay. Two observations are in order. First, it is striking just how readily *both* cases can be made in this debate. Forms of association are so myriad—everything from bar associations to bowling teams—and conceptual terms are so fluid—is a barbecue a family event or neighboring?—that enormous quantities of data can be pitched from both sides. Perhaps that is why so much of the debate seems like an intellectual snowball fight with lots of glittering pieces flying back and forth but precious few direct hits. Observation two concerns what the aforementioned sentence calls the "terms of the debate." The clash of data, such as it is, concerns the *overall direction* of social life in America, and the answer to a simple question: Is it up *or* down? In his history of American civic life, Michael Schudson observes that, "The rhetoric of decline should send up a red flag; for the socially-concerned intellectual, it is an off-the-rack rhetoric..."[16] Perhaps what is at issue here is more than a simple up/down question.

Imagine performing an insect census for your garden. It is a daunting task. The raw quantity of insects is huge, and they are not presenting themselves for enumeration. There are further complications. A single ant colony can number in the millions, whereas bees and butterflies may only visit by the hundreds, tens or singles. To make any sense of it at all, one must apply some classification scheme—a taxonomy—to be sure the major species are being properly counted. But even if one has identified the major species and found a technique to reveal their numbers (digging around stones or counting bugs on a particular flower, for example), there is still the matter of ecology. Lurking behind every species count is the connection of that number to a number of other species. Ants and bees are competitors, and both are food for spiders who are prey for wasps also eaten by spiders. The garden contains a dynamic balance of complex linkages. That is what an ecology *is*.

Let us make the analogy explicit: "A food web is a network much like a social community... with species linked to one another in a tangled pattern..."[17] Tangled indeed. Studies of even small ecologies find interspecies links in the many thousands; imagine the complexity of the interplay among the clubs, co-workers and churches in a single human community, let alone across a whole society. Moreover, the health of a garden/human community need not be judged by simple counts of species/associations. What makes either a "community" is the very interplay between living elements that renders aggregate counts so problematic.

It is time to dispense with analogies and to introduce a sociological concept: *Social capital is the social structures that individuals build and maintain to seek the things they value.* It is a concept with a relatively recent but distinguished lineage which will be addressed in Chapter 2. But the central mission of this book is not just to conceptualize social capital, but rather to assess its value in America. Can it be done?

The answer is yes. What is required (as with our insect census) is a taxonomy explicitly laying out the major forms of social capital, *and* the pattern of their interrelationships (as in the food web of an ecology). The schematic diagram below is the working model of social capital:

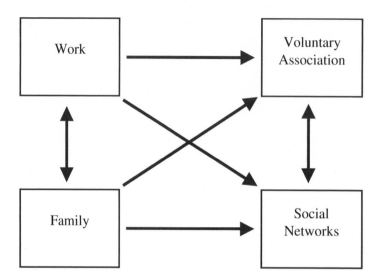

Figure 1.1

Chapters 3 through 6 address the content of each of the four boxes in turn. First, a General Patterns section will lay out levels of, for instance, Social Network contact, both overall and broken down by sex, age and education; second, a Societal Trends section will track those patterns through the early 1970s to the year 2000. Chapters 7 and 8 will then add substance to the arrows connecting the boxes.

Attention to such arrows is indispensable, and not just for the ecologist. Of course, if one is only interested in whether, say, Voluntary Association membership is up or down over the past generation, then it may be necessary to keep the arrows in the background because everybody knows that families, friends and careers affect the groups people join. But if the issue extends beyond a census of separate boxes to the living pattern of the garden/community, the arrows jump right into the foreground. How do real people put together their lives by balancing their social commitments? What do recent increases in divorce and work hours do to the overall social pattern? These are not simple up/down questions.

Answers cannot come from analogies or ad hoc examples. What is required is data about "real people." Two major sources will be used to fill in the blanks of the social capital model. The General Social Survey (GSS) is one of the most widely used data sources in modern sociology. It is the gold standard for survey research, utilizing multistage sampling techniques to draw a cross-section of America, and addressing a battery of questions about their attitudes and behaviors to Americans in a personal interview format. Moreover, the GSS offers a long-term record of our social history. It has been conducted 23 times since between 1972 and 2000, thus spanning a three-decade interval that should be ample for spotting model trends.[18] A secondary data source will be the Social Capital Community Benchmark Survey 2000 (SCCBS 2000), composed of both a national sample of 3,000 respondents, and separate samples of 41 communities in the U.S. providing an additional 26,700 respondents. The latter was designed by Robert Putnam and his Saguaro Seminar group, and it provides lush detail about myriad forms of social contact. SCCBS 2000 offers current breadth of information to supplement the historical depth of the GSS.[19]

Now that its subject has been (literally) drawn, a word about the subtitle of this book. "Treasure" is a play on the word "capital" highlighting its value. The truth requires no highlights. Putnam, the civic task forces and concerned Americans are all dead right that if social capital *is* down, we all lose. In a real sense, Figure 1.1 is a close-up picture of American society itself; if its vitality suffers, we all suffer. The stock phrase "American society" elicits the image of a capitalist, democratic superpower. Buried beneath these public institutions is the trove of social bonds we tend everyday. They are the treasures to be unearthed in the chapters to follow.

LOOKING BACKWARD

I am writing this section on January 1, 2010. The dawn of a new decade throws into bold relief a question that could occur to the readers in Chapter 3 concerning work: Why does the timeline of the present analysis stop in the year 2000?

There are three reasons.

First, the very foundation of the entire analysis is the model of social capital itself. The "lush detail" of data in the SCCBS 2000 dataset—and its parallelism to the 2000 GSS—affords a unique opportunity to lay bare the underlying framework of America's social life. Without a firmly founded diagram of that structure, one tends to get caught in the inconclusive snowball fight about social capital described above.

The second reason for tracking trends from the Seventies through the Nineties can be simply put: this account takes the long view. Who would not agree that trends in social capital in the Aughts are firmly rooted in America's path through the latter decades of the 20th century? Rapid-fire media news cycles tend to focus on this year's data, but the present analysis is built precisely to screen out short-term fluctuations. Decade-by-decade timelines offer a more reliable path through America's social history.

The final reason is the most simply put of all: the new century is to be analyzed in a new book. The successor volume to *Social Capital in America* will bring the account up to date by encompassing all available GSS data for the new decade.

2

Designing a Model of
Social Capital

> I consider man as formed for
> society with those dispositions
> which fit him for society.
> —*Thomas Jefferson*

THE MARCH OF AN IDEA

Given his role in the invention of America, it seems only right and proper to open this chapter with Jefferson's meditation on the nature of "man" (*sic*, and woman) and society. Unfortunately, in the days of the Founding Fathers (*sic*, and Mothers, too) it remained a meditation. Philosophical ruminations could not be checked against the fact-machine of modern social science. But there are limits, of course, to raw computer-driven empiricism. Everything-but-the-kitchen-sink data deployments of anything that looks like social capital have been harshly criticized by, among others, yours truly. What is required is proper conceptualization: a careful determination of the key components of social capital before the numbers start to fly.

The rationale behind the opening quote is that social capital is something central to society *and* self. That idea and a sense of American distinctiveness resonated through the generation after Jefferson in the famous words of a non-American:

> The political associations that exist in the United States are only a single feature in the midst of the immense assemblage of associations in that country. Americans of all ages, all conditions, and all dispositions constantly form associations. They have not only commercial and manufacturing companies, in which all take part, but associations of a thousand other kinds, religious, moral, serious, futile, general or restricted, enormous or diminutive. The Americans make associations to give entertainments, to found seminaries, to build inns, to construct churches, to diffuse books, to send missionaries to the antipodes; in this manner they found hospitals, prisons, and schools. If it is proposed to inculcate some truth or foster some feeling by the

encouragement of a great example, they form a society. Wherever at the head of some new undertaking you see the government in France, or a man of rank in England, in the United States you will be sure to find an association.[1]

Thus spoke Alexis de Tocqueville, who further pronounced us a "nation of join-ers." All the scarier, then, if this fundamental feature of America has been lost.

Tocqueville's spotlighting of the crucial social structures operating in the zone between state and self has made him the "patron saint of contemporary social capitalists." The currency of the concept in modern social science is often traced to James Coleman's much-cited 1988 definition:

> Social capital is defined by its function. It is not a single entity but a varie-ty of different entities, with two elements in common: they all consist of some aspect of social structures, and they facilitate certain actions of actors... within the structure... Like other forms of capital, social capital is productive, making possible the achievement of certain ends that in its absence would not be possi-ble.[2]

Coleman referred to social capital as "the connective tissue" of society. The conviction that it is the very flesh-and-blood of social life swept through the human sciences starting in the mid-1990s. Social capital was the subject of liter-ally hundreds of new articles since 1994, making it that "...rare concept indeed that excites simultaneous interest across political science, economics, sociology, criminology, psychology, [and] education..."[3]

Nor has the surge of interest in social capital stopped at the ivy-covered walls of the academy. According to the widely admired literature review on the topic written by Alejandro Portes (former president of the American Sociologi-cal Association), "...the concept of social capital has become one of the most popular exports from sociological theory into popular language."[4] Robert Put-nam's version of the concept earned him a profile in no less popular an outlet than *People* magazine. Putnam's ideas also made it into President Clinton's State of the Union address in 1995, then crossed the political aisle into President Bush's State of the Union address in 2002.[5] Former Prime Minister Tony Blair of Great Britain has referred to social capital in policy speeches, and interna-tional organizations such as the Organisation for Economic Co-Operation & Development and the World Bank are developing measures of it.[6] Social capital has penetrated the consciousness of professors, policy-makers, and the public. So what is it?

ON THE MEANING OF SOCIAL CAPITAL

Not all of the fanfare surrounding this concept has been positive. One book on the subject calls it "...a totally chaotic, ambiguous, and general category that can be viewed as a notional umbrella for almost any purpose."[7] Another social capi-tal author says that "...in many research and policy papers, the issue of what counts as social capital is implicit and often confused."[8] This chapter aims to dispel that confusion by clearly stipulating the conceptual underpinnings of so-cial capital.

But before assembling the scholarly sources of the present model, let us en-gage in a common-sensical exercise. Consider the pop culture (and increasingly annoying) phrase, "Get a life." What does it mean? It seems to be a prompt to do something meaningful with your time—get a job, find a husband, join a gym, visit a friend... Each of these actions is an appropriate response to the catch-phrase, and each touches one of the four zones depicted in Figure 1.1. Those conceptual boxes now need to be filled with more intellectual substance than a throwaway line on a sitcom can provide.

Two points should overview the discussion of the model's design. First, the theoretical grounding will work through current scholarship, but also reach back to the founders of sociology itself. The classical theorists of the discipline—Emile Durkheim, Karl Marx and Max Weber—grappled with fundamental is-sues about the founding of modern societies such as the USA. As Portes puts it so elegantly, "Tracing the intellectual background of the concept into classical times would be paramount to revisiting sociology's major 19th century sources."[9] So we shall.

A second prefatory point concerns the need for all of this documentation. It would seem that so high-profile an idea, a concept that has broken through to enter into everyday public discourse, would have a recognizable referent. Should not the shape of social capital be, well, obvious? By way of answer, consider the insight of anthropologist Mary Douglas, "...that institutions, once created, fade from view to work automatically on our behalf."[10] Churches, scout troops, and crime watch groups are operating in your neighborhood right now whether you are aware of it or not; you are certainly not aware of the totality of such local activity. Even more certain is that people have no tally in their heads of *all* such activity for the USA as a whole. It is out there, but has "fade[d] from view" un-der the accumulated business of daily life. Now is the time to dig social capital up.

COMPONENTS OF THE MODEL

Voluntary Association

For the attribution of the origin and popularization of this term, all eyes turn to Alexis de Tocqueville and his magisterial work *Democracy in America*. Al-though the word "voluntary" is not mentioned in the quotation on page 8, the whole thrust of Tocqueville's analysis concerns the distinctively American re-sponse to freely "form a group" rather than to rely on oneself or one's govern-ment.

The clearest kinship with these ideas is shared by Emile Durkheim, Toc-queville's countryman and the putative Founding Father of sociology. Durk-heim's statement about the present component of social capital speaks of neces-sity rather than distinctiveness:

> A nation can be maintained *only if*, between the state and the individual, there is interposed a whole series of secondary groups near enough to the individuals to attract them strongly in their sphere of action and drag them, in this way, into the general torrent of social life [emphasis added].[11]

It is a commonplace of the literature that Tocqueville and Durkheim both raised the profile of the "intermediate domains of social life" referred to as voluntary association.[12]

Karl Marx, by contrast, had his analytical eye on structures and processes operating at the very highest level of society, and even across societies. In sketching out the rise of industrial capitalism, patterns of neighborhood joining tended to fade into the background. Nevertheless, there are aspects of Marx's analysis readily brought into the foreground as voluntary association:

> ...the growth of large factories brings workers together in one place, where it is easier for them to organize. Capitalist development centralizes production in large cities; the large numbers of rural workers once separated in small villages and factory towns, now acquire political strength from urbanization. As large monopolistic businesses supplant smaller ones, they actually draw the communications and transportation networks of society more tightly together. The end result is to prepare the way organizationally for socialism.[13]

So: the massive movements of industrial capital laid the groundwork for smaller-scale forms of social capital serving economic self-interest—unions, professional associations, presumably even churches in which to ingest the "opiate of the people."

Max Weber likewise favored grand theory. Conceptualizing bureaucracy, the organizational centerpiece of the modern age, means operating at the level of true macrostructures. The present model frames microstructures, which means individual-level social connections. But again there are important theoretical threads trailing down to social capital ground level. In *The Protestant Ethic and the Spirit of Capitalism*,[14] perhaps Weber's grandest work, he mounts an argument that churches—voluntary associations *par excellence*—played a role in the rise of modern society itself. In the essay "The Protestant Sects and the Spirit of Capitalism," Weber calls denominational churches the "prototype of voluntary associations," and further argues that they bred the work ethic of modern capitalism in America.[15] Elsewhere in his work on social stratification in modern societies Weber refers to class-based groups (e.g., unions), status groups (e.g., ethnic clubs), and political groups (e.g., campaign committees) that clearly belong in the voluntary association box.[16]

Family

It seems perfectly apt (even obvious) to include a social structure often referred to as the "foundation" or "building block" of society in a section on modular components. Durkheim says that "...Society was originally organized on the family basis."[17] Foundation, indeed. Nor has its value as social capital diminished. In their essay on civil society following Durkheim's analysis of "mediating structures," Peter Berger and Richard Neuhaus assert the opposite:

> ...Modernization has already had a major impact on the family. It has largely stripped the family of earlier functions in the areas of education and economics, for example. But in other ways, modernization has made the family more important than ever before. It is the major institution within the private sphere, and thus for many people, the most valuable thing in their lives. Here they make their moral commitments, invest their emotions, plan for the future, and perhaps even hope for immortality.[18]

Building block, indeed.

The family's status as a fundamental form of social capital would seem beyond argument. Moreover, it is compatible with virtually every theoretical definition of social capital, certainly including Coleman's conceptualization stated earlier. And even though Coleman did develop a family-based explanation of parochial school achievement, the family is conspicuously absent from many other analytical models of social capital.[19] In *Bowling Alone*, Putnam actually considers changes in family life, including single-parent households and women working, as potential reasons for the decline of other, presumably more fundamental, forms of social capital. This is a perfectly reasonable empirical question, but it seems even more reasonable to keep the family inside the picture. In the language of economic analysis, the present model conceptualizes the family as an endogenous—i.e., inner—component of social capital distinct from exogenous—i.e., outer—factors in society.

This position is documented in a remarkable article by Astone et al. entitled, "Family Demography, Social Theory and Investment in Social Capital." After conducting their own formidable literature review, the authors broadly assert that "...family formation is among the most important types of investment in social capital made in all societies."[20] If these investments are declining in America, that is certainly a net capital loss which could hardly help but affect other social structures. Astone et al. also refine the present conceptualization of the family component in the following statement: "Family behaviors, including marriage and childbearing, remain the classic examples of investment in social capital."[21] The model will measure precisely those two behaviors as investment inputs into family life.

Social Networks

Evidence of the treasures buried in personal relationships stretches back to the dawn of the discipline in Durkheim's seminal work *Suicide*, which showed the protective effects of interaction. But it was in the 1970s that sociology hit the motherlode with the formalization of the concept of the social network.

One excellent introductory textbook defines the term as "the pattern of ties among the units in a social system."[22] In the present application, those "ties" are interpersonal relationships and the "units" are individuals. So many studies have cast up findings of networks' personal benefits that the same textbook classifies them by properly Jeffersonian categories: "Life" (evidence of network effects on morbity and mortality)... "liberty" (evidence that networks influence migration patterns and job-finding in "The Land of the Free")...and the "pursuit of happiness" (evidence that networks impact personal psychological patterns by providing social support).[23]

One very influential practitioner of social network analysis has recently written a book entitled *Social Capital*. Nan Lin's definition of the latter term is "resources embedded in social networks and used by actors for actions."[24] Essentially, Lin would use social networks as the master concept underlying all forms of capital. The present formulation is more modest, conceptually distinguishing patterns of interpersonal interaction with friends, kin and neighbors from the other components of social capital.

Work

At least one Founding Father considered work a font of moral worthiness (Ben Franklin); the founder of modern psychiatry called it one of "the cornerstones of our humanness" (see the banner of Chapter 3). But in the contemporary analytics of social capital, there is some distrust of work in America. In *Bowling Alone*, Putnam says:

> ..."work" entails time and effort destined to serve primarily material, not social, ends. Work-based networks are often used for instrumental purposes, thus somewhat undercutting their value for community and social purposes.[25]

Frankly, this would seem to be another empirical question, especially since Putnam later concedes that "Civic engagement and social connectedness can be found inside the workplace..."[26] So we shall see. It seems decidedly odd to exclude work because of its unsavoriness while in his chapter called "The Dark Side of Social Capital," the Klu Klux Klan does qualify for the designation. The present decision is to formally add work to the model of social capital, if only for purposes of empirical demonstration. As will become immediately apparent, however, there is much more substance to the decision than that. In fact, let us turn now to four good reasons for the inclusion of work as an endogenous factor in the model.

1. WORK IS SOCIAL. With rare exceptions, time spent on the job is time spent interacting with other people. Forest rangers in the Alaskan wilderness must deal with poachers and government officials; nerdy web designers still have to negotiate with clients and attend occasional software seminars. For most of the rest of us, the point is even more self-evident. College professing may seem to be a life of solitary scholarship and lecturing from a podium, but this is a sham. Behind the departmental door are snubs by secretaries, frayed authority relations with chairpersons, poor social skills hampering team-taught courses and toxic office politics leading to departmental meeting shouting matches. In other words, the usual stuff of social life.

2. WORK IS CAPITAL. In his encyclopedic recent volume *Social Capital,* David Halpern boldly states that, "It can be argued—rather convincingly—that one of the most common and important forms of social capital is the firm or company."[27] This is hard to deny given the cliché, "The business of America is business," but there is the potential here for conceptual confusion.

Corporations are, of course, large-scale bureaucracies with towering hierarchies and multinational reach. In other words, macrostructures. But the individual worker—even the C.E.O.—encounters the job at the level of the office or work team. In other words, in a microstructure. The fact that both levels of the structure occupy the same address should not preclude the addition of work as a model component.

Clearly, what is being attempted here is not a comparative organizational analysis of bureaucratic types. The focus, rather, is on the social commitment of individuals to the job. Specifically, there are clear advantages to the company of a well-organized office:

> Better knowledge sharing, due to established trust relationships, common frames of reference, and shared goals.

> Greater coherence of action due to organizational stability and shared understanding.

> Lower transaction costs, due to a high level of trust and a cooperative spirit (both within the organization and between the organization and its customers and partners).[28]

Of course, the individual worker receives a return from these advantages as well. Benefits accrue to both the macrostructure and the microstructure; the present model will only consider the latter. The personal investment of work time with the hope of future payoff in a productive career would seem to be the very definition of the term "capital."

3. WORK IS CONNECTED TO OTHER FORMS OF SOCIAL CAPITAL. As mentioned above, this is really an empirical question to be addressed in the chapters to follow. All that is needed here is a *prima facie* case of the linkages between work and the other capital components.

Note in Figure 1.1 that the hypothesized effect arrows emanate *from* work *to* voluntary association and social networks. Part of the reason for not pointing the arrows back the other way is that those effects have already been densely documented. Weber's famous essay on Protestant churches in America described them as voluntary associations in which individuals could demonstrate the stern discipline that would translate into a work ethic—church membership as a kind of job internship. It is well-known that the conferences of professional associations are also job fairs. Even though their membership and influence has slipped in the USA, unions still impact work processes and job placement.

One of the major reasons for the rise of social networks as a sociological concept and as a recognized form of social capital is precisely their proven effect on job flows. Hundreds of studies (including some by this author) have

shown that informal social contacts do lead to jobs. In his review of this literature, Portes extends the point to research on ethnic business enclaves. Through
ethnically based social ties, local labor forces are stocked in places like New
York's Chinatown and Miami's Little Havana; such network concentrations
have also kept ethnic outsiders out of the construction trades and diamond business in New York.[29]

Here is the point: if voluntary associations and social networks exert such
pervasive effects on work, *it is implausible that there should be no feedback
effects*. If a union gets someone a job, is that not likely to strengthen that person's membership loyalty and, indeed, convince others to join? If a friend gets
you a job, should that not cement the friendship?

In his book on *Civil Society*, John Ehrenberg puts the point more forcefully:

> The economy is not just another sphere of association like a book group,
> bowling league, or block association. It is an extraordinarily powerful set of so-
> cial relations whose imperatives are penetrating and organizing ever-wider
> areas of public and private life.[30]

Whether or not work is the dominant form of social capital, it certainly has the
prima facie credentials to be considered as a model component.

4. CLASSICAL CONSIDERATIONS ON HUMAN LABOR. Tracing these
ideas back to the start of sociology is not just some exercise in scholasticism, of
dutifully footnoting the founders. In the present case, it banishes all doubt about
the proper place of work in the research model.

The most direct demonstration of work's relevance is in Marx's theoretical
insight that the key to modern social organization is the relationship between
capitalists and workers. This insight is developed in the conceptualization of
Pierre Bourdieu, who "...explicitly incorporates into his definition the Marxist
idea that the raw material that produces a capital resource is always, at its ulti-
mate origin, human labor."[31] So: not only does work make social capital, but it is
also the very basis of economic, human and cultural capital as well.

Weber's position can be succinctly re-summarized. Protestant denomina-
tions planted the seed of the Protestant work ethic, which bloomed forth into
capitalist industrial organization. If modern work habits figured into the origin
of modern society itself, it would seem surpassingly strange to exclude work
from Figure 1.1.

But the classical theorist who most explicitly addressed work in the modern
age and conceptualized it most clearly as social capital was Durkheim. Essentially, he was concerned about the decline of social solidarity occasioned by the
transformation of agrarian into industrial societies. In the preface to *The Division of Labor in Society*, Durkheim seems to dismiss current concerns about the
unsavoriness of corporate work:

> ...these origins do not justify our attributing to it that kind of constitution-
> ally amoral state with which we gratuitously credit it. Just as the family had
> been the environment within which domestic morality and law had been
> worked out, so the corporation was the natural environment within which pro-
> fessional morality and law had to be elaborated.[32]

Clearly, work sites are not to be viewed as staging areas for amoral individualism. The passing of traditional family life creates a moral gap to be filled by occupationally based groupings:

> Such causes [of social solidarity] are not peculiar to the family but are to be found, although in different forms, within the corporation. Thus if the former group has played so important a role in the moral history of humanity, why should not the latter be capable of so doing?[33]

Now, to be fair, it is sometimes unclear whether Durkheim's vision describes the modern corporation or occupational associations that would enroll all members of a profession. Either way, in an 1893 book Durkheim comes remarkably close to defining work as a potential wellspring of social capital.

CONCLUDING ISSUES

Elaborating the Model

Assessing the values and charting the flows among the four components of social capital would seem to be a substantial—and, I shall argue, original—body of work. As every grizzled data analyst knows, however, one must beware simplicity. Neglect of complicating factors outside the paradigm proper can lead to disastrously misleading results. That is why the research model will be elaborated by the routine consideration of sex, age, education, and race.

Before substantively justifying those variables, there is need of a methodological note. "Routine consideration" generally means statistical control, which can assume two basic forms. In regression-style analyses, one typically "partials out" the effects of the control variables to highlight the unique influence of the independent variables of interest. So a multiple regression looking at how work affects group membership, say, might include controls for sex and age. In effect, this pulls out the influence of those controls to see the pure impact of work on voluntary association. This approach especially makes sense when the influence of the controls on the dependent variable (in this instance, groups) is already well-known. A second form of statistical control essentially runs separate analyses *within* the categories of the controls. That way one can observe how the effects differ for males and females rather than removing sex effects entirely. This is especially sensible in cases like the present one in which a new model is being developed. To emphasize that the knowledge base is *not* so highly developed that they can be statistically waved aside, the chapters will directly display in crosstabulations the levels of each social capital component by sex, age, education and race (in General Patterns), then use them again to break down changes over time (in Societal Trends).

When the model of social capital has been assembled and applied (Chapters 7, 8, 9 and 10), the statistical technique of choice is multivariate analysis of variance (MANOVA). It sounds forbidding, but one of MANOVA's strengths in the present application is its transparency to nonspecialists. It uses the second form of statistical control just described, and is amenable to visual display for several variables. A quick glance at Figure 7.2 (in Chapter 7), for instance, clearly shows the effects of one form of social capital on another for males and females, and for different age groups as well. The pretty pictures are backed up by statistical tests from the same family as multiple regression analysis, which is widely used by social capital scholars.[34] An additional advantage of MANOVA, though, is that it allows for routine tests of interaction effects. This means that if the effect differs for, say, males vs. females, it will be reflected in the statistical values as well as in the drawings.

Education is the darling of what are known as "human capital" theories in economics. They are so-called because they concern investment in skills that have some pragmatic payoff in salary or upward mobility. Of course in modern American life the choice to do something as expensive and time-consuming as college is motivated by the fact that it is a blue-chip form of human capital. To Durkheim, theorizing nearly a century in advance of these theories, education has loftier, more "human" purposes. His first academic position was at France's first teacher's college, where he oversaw numerous reforms of the educational system. In an essay entitled, "Education: Its Nature and Its Role," he speaks of society's responsibility to the next generation:

> To the egotistic and asocial being that has just been born it must, as rapid-
> ly as possible add another, capable of leading a moral and social life. Such is
> the work of education...[35]

The "final goal of moral education" is "to attach the child to these groups... to which he belongs." Durkheim even likened lay teachers to priests in their authority. Pretty lofty stuff.[36]

There is no need to treat Durkheim as some sort of seer on the modern role of education. We now have the data:

> Virtually every piece of empirical research on social capital has concluded
> that education, and particularly university education, is associated with higher
> levels of social capital at the individual level.[37]

Given its social profitability and theoretical grounding, it seems essential to keep education in the foreground of analyses of social capital. Yet Putnam and others, somewhat mysteriously, do not.[38] By using the first form of statistical control described above, they simply screen out the effects of education to spotlight other factors. In important respects, level of education will actually *become* the spotlight for illuminating social capital in the chapters to follow.

Since very early in the development of the concept, racial differences in social capital have been the subject of speculation, and even some empirical demonstration. Economist Glen Loury pointed to capital deficits among minorities two decades ago, [39] and Alejandro Portes' literature review cited above has compiled evidence on "ethnic business enclaves" linking social networks to work.

In general, though, race has entered this literature in highly specialized studies (such as racial contrasts in parental effects on schooling) or, again, as a control variable in global analyses (such as *Bowling Alone*). Consequently, there is much we do not know about basic racial differences in social capital:

> ...even when the importance of race is forcefully acknowledged, it is not fully or appropriately incorporated into the empirical analysis. Specifically, social capital studies focus on overall outcomes and indicators; they do not disaggregate data in a way that permits analysis of relative, racially specific effects... In other words, the treatment of race in America within the social capital thesis, and hence its understanding of American civil society, is incomplete.[40]

The present analysis will signal its agreement with this assessment by "disaggregat(ing) data" in the simplest, most direct way: showing comparative capital accounts for blacks and whites. Race will be a standard variable in the General Patterns tables to come. Race tables will not, however, be included in the Societal Trends sections of the middle chapters for two reasons: 1. black-white social changes over this time period are so complexly intertwined with education as to be actively misleading if viewed by race alone and, consequently, 2. these changes are to be featured in a full chapter of their own (Chapter 9).

The other two variables fleshing out the model of social capital are sex and age. These are two of the standard "demographics" used to break down every commercial and academic survey. The reason for this routine inclusion, of course, is that they are important sources of variation across a vast range of variables. There are impressive literatures suggesting that men and women differ in many forms of civic engagement; the *prima facie* case for age is equally impressive.[41] Those differences will be specifically tested in the social capital comparisons below.

MASTER PLAN OF THE BOOK

To stick with the metaphor of design, specifications on the modular components must be complete before drawing the full blueprint. Chapters 3 through 6 will therefore focus on each of the four dimensions of social capital in turn. Chapter 7 is devoted to sketching the complex interconnections among the components, a kind of sociological reverse engineering. Once the basic structure of the model has been sketched, the issue of modification over time is to be addressed in Chapter 8. Chapter 9 will then use the "full blueprint" to interpret overall trends with an eye to social inequality indexed by education and race. Finally, Chapter 10 will consider the exogenous impact of two forms of media technology—television and the internet—about which lavish claims have been made concerning the future of social capital in America.

3

WORK

> Love and work are the cornerstones of our
> humanness.
> —*Sigmund Freud*

Current accounts of work in America cast it as corrosive to both love *and* humanness. Consider some recent titles:

> Diane Fassel, *Working Ourselves to Death: The High Costs of
> Workaholism and The Rewards of Recovery.*
> Bryan E. Robinson, *Chained to the Desk: A Guide for Workaholics, Their
> Partners and Children, and the Clinicians Who Treat Them.*
> Paul Thorne and Michael Johnson, *Getting a Life in the Killing Fields of
> Work.*[1]

References to work involving addiction, chains, and even killing fields are hard to reconcile with the American tradition of the Protestant work ethic. Now consider some revered references from a pre-Freudian (and even pre-Tocquevilleian) cultural commentator—Poor Richard:

> God gives all things to industry, then plough deep, while sluggards sleep...
> There will be sleeping enough in the grave...
> Be ashamed to catch yourself idle...
> God helps those that help themselves...[2]

The message of Benjamin Franklin's 1757 essay "The Way to Wealth" is clear: work is not only the way to wealth, it is the way to moral worthiness.

Good or bad, work appears to be gaining ground in the way Americans actually live their lives. Juliet B. Schor's 1992 book *The Overworked American* spotlighted the upward trend in work that is the backdrop for the newer titles on work pathology:

> My estimates... confirm not only that more people are working, but that
> they are working more... The rise of worktime was unexpected. For nearly a
> hundred years, hours had been declining... But the change was barely noticed.
> Equally surprising, but also hardly recognized, has been the deviation from

19

Western Europe. After progressing in tandem for nearly a century, the United States veered off into a trajectory of declining leisure... [3]

Current international comparisons are instructive in their simplicity. *The State of Working America 2002/2003* report of the Economic Policy Institute states it unequivocally:

> The U.S. economy employs a greater share of its working-age population, and its workers work, on average, more hours per year, than is the case in any other rich, industrialized economy. [4]

We *increased* our work hours over 1979-2000 while Japan, Germany and France *decreased* theirs by hundreds of hours per year.

So: Americans appear to be the hardest-working people in the First World, with their noses ever longer at the grindstone. So what? To analysts who consider work a form of social capital (a *prima facie* case just made in Chapter 2), this means an appreciation of societal riches. To others, work is a form of fool's gold that glitters only as a temptation to selfish individualism. Indeed, in surveying the potential causes of his aggregate decline of social capital in America, Robert Putnam wonders if, "Perhaps the villain of the piece is simply overwork." [5]

GENERAL PATTERNS

The present account, of course, does not begin with "aggregate declines," then probe backwards to find "villains." Quite the reverse. My approach is to break down the assets of each type of social capital before evaluating the whole portfolio.

Sex

An overview of work assets in contemporary America is displayed in Table 3.1. Note immediately that labor force participation is separately exhibited for males (top row) and females (bottom row); to unpack the information in the General Patterns tables, therefore, simply look down each column to see a direct comparison. Performing this operation for the first column shows that just over 70% of American males and just under 60% of American females are actively in the labor force. This placed the USA first in the fraction of female employment among comparable nations, and a narrow second in the male fraction (about one percentage point behind Japan). [6] Given that the Social Capital Community Benchmark Survey (which will be the source throughout these General Patterns) is a 2000 dataset, note the relatively rosy—but comparable—male/female unemployment figures. Note also that the male/female figures for "Homemaker" are *not* comparable. With respect to the relatively modest 12.1% of American females who circle that status, stay-at-home-husband/"Mr. Moms" are a vanishingly small percentage of American males (0.6%).

Table 3.1 Labor Force Participation for males and females

| | Labor Force Participation | | | | | | |
	Working	Laid Off	Unem-ployed	Retired	Permanent Disability	Home-maker	Student
Males	71.0%	2.1%	2.8%	16.2%	3.2%	0.6%	4.1%
Females	57.6%	1.7%	3.0%	18.2%	3.5%	12.1%	3.9%

n = 29,161

Table 3.2 further breaks down labor force participation into hours worked by respondents.7 This is the real index of just how hard-working Americans are. The figures in the 0 hours per week column are what one would have expected given Table 3.1. The "part-time" work segments of 1-20 and 21-39 hours are relatively small percentages of the workforce, with somewhat greater participation rates for women than for men (7.2% vs. 3.3% for 1-20 hours; 10.5% vs. 5.0% for 21-39 hours, respectively). Much smaller than expectations are the fractions working traditional, "full time" 40-hour work weeks; only one-fifth of women show that level of work participation, and even fewer men. In fact, nearly twice as many males work 41-60 hours as work the traditional full-time stint (37.0% vs. 18.9%); for females, the 40 and 41-60 hour segments are about the same (20.0% vs. 19.3%). Finally, the 61+ hour slice represents about one of every twelve men, and about one of every thirty-three women. Purely by the numbers, there really are millions of American workaholics—of both sexes.

Table 3.2 Hours Worked by males and females

| | Hours Worked | | | | | |
	0	1-20	21-39	40	41-60	61+
Males	27.2%	3.3%	5.0%	18.9%	37.0%	8.6%
Females	39.7%	7.2%	10.5%	20.0%	19.3%	3.3%

n = 29,050

Age

Sociology 101 defines sex as an *ascribed* trait, that is, a personal characteristic that is inherited and involuntary.[8] Ascribed are distinguished from achieved traits that are, well, achieved by merit and effort. The distinction is a useful one, especially when it comes to relating one trait to the other. Ascription by sex used to preclude female achievement at work, while requiring it of males. Tribal societies were ascriptively "age graded" such that all individual age-mates were engaged with—or disengaged from—a given economic task. To what degree is work in contemporary America age-graded?

To a substantial degree. Turn directly to Table 3.3, and notice how bottom-heavy the left-hand column is; a full 60% of Americans 50 years and older work no hours at all. Of course many of these folks are retired, a form of age-grading to be re-examined under Societal Trends. For analytical purposes, age 65+ was not broken out from the 50+ category shown here. First of all, this permits a consistent comparison of tripartite age categories across the various forms of social capital. Second, it does not tip the hand in Societal Trends too much to say that early retirements and Walmart employee elders make 65+ a bit of a leaky age-work boundary.

Table 3.3 Hours Worked by younger, middle-aged and older adults

	Hours Worked					
	0	1-20	21-39	40	41-60	61+
< 30	22.2%	8.4%	12.1%	23.7%	27.2%	6.4%
30-49	17.2%	5.0%	7.7%	23.8%	38.4%	7.9%
50+	59.9%	3.6%	5.6%	11.5%	16.3%	3.1%

n = 28,324

Staying with the present age breakdown, then, about one out of six age 50+ adults work 41-60 hours per week (16.3%), and about one in nine do the old-fashioned work week (11.5% for 40 hours). Both of these figures more than double for the middle-aged workers shown in the middle row, who also have the highest fraction of 61+ hours workers (7.9%). The younger workers in the top row are a bit above mid-life workers in the sub-40 hours categories, and a bit below them from forty hours on up. As an ascribed trait, age does indeed grade participation levels in the achieved arena of work.[9]

Education

As parents tell their kids, this is the most influential "achieved" trait in societies such as modern America. Moreover, education is the darling of both human capital theories in economics and intergenerational mobility models in sociology. Both intellectual frameworks relate educational achievement to occupational achievement, a path that must pass through hours worked.

Does it ever. A comparison of the top and bottom rows in Table 3.4 shows that adults lacking a high school degree are roughly *twice* as likely to not be

Table 3.4 Hours Worked by level of education

	Hours Worked					
	0	1-20	21-39	40	41-60	61+
Less than high school	55.3%	4.9%	5.2%	15.4%	14.1%	5.0%
High school	39.5%	4.3%	7.7%	20.3%	22.3%	5.8%
College	27.0%	5.8%	8.5%	19.8%	33.0%	6.0%

n = 28,708

working at all (55.3%) as the college-educated (27.0%), with high school grads right in-between (39.5%). Naturally this means that more educated Americans will be overrepresented at higher levels of work effort, as indeed they are. The fraction of 41-60 hours workers descends from 33.0% to 22.3% to 14.1% at each lower educational rung. More education may translate into more success, but it definitely translates into more time at the grindstone.[10]

Race

The black-white comparison in work profiles offered in Table 3.5 yields only a single notable difference. Black Americans are significantly more likely to occupy the traditional "full time" category (24.2% to 17.3% for whites) whereas white workers report a higher percentage for 41-60 hours (29.5% to 23.3% for black workers).

Table 3.5 Hours Worked by race

	Hours Worked					
	0	1-20	21-39	40	41-60	61+
White	34.4%	5.3%	7.9%	17.3%	29.5%	5.7%
Black	32.9%	4.8%	8.4%	24.2%	23.3%	6.5%

n = 23,985

SOCIETAL TRENDS

It is time for a brief meditation on this book's subtitle. In the course of their day-to-day living, people make lots of seemingly small decisions about the use of their time. If I go to church, can I pick up the family laundry before the cleaners close? Should I stay late at work, or get to the kids' soccer game? It's visiting day at Mom's nursing home, but my buddies want to go bowling...

Such choices add up to separate accounts in our "four zones" of social capital, *but who is aware of that?* Who keeps a running tally of social commitments made (or broken) in their own lives, let alone in the lives of their fellow Americans? Most people are not even aware how many hours they personally worked last week unless a survey researcher asks them. Contributions to the "treasure" of social capital remain "buried" beneath the business of living. Here, the trove of work hours has been unearthed and arranged in the neat little piles called General Patterns, but there is a complication. The tables above are snapshots taken in 2000 of the moving picture that is American life. A proper accounting of social capital must chart changes over time, just as cost accounting does.

So as the General Social Survey tables unroll below, the recurrent question will be *how much of a decade-to-decade change constitutes real change?* Even state-of-the-art samples like the GSS must accept a certain amount of sampling error. The rule of thumb to be applied is a 5% shift. It is an intuitively appealing standard that is about twice as large as the error for a national survey of 1,500 respondents. More rigorous statistical tests for specialists will be routinely re-ported in the Notes.[11]

Sex

This section charts social changes in work in America. The site of greatest change is Table 3.6b, wherein working women went from a clear minority to a clear majority. The lowering of sex as an ascribed barrier to work achievement is dramatically demonstrated in the shrinkage of the no (0) work hours column from 63.0% to 42.2% of American women. Relatively few of these tens of mil-lions of women have entered the labor force at the low end. The part-time cate-gories grew only a few percentage points from the Seventies through the Nine-ties (6.2% to 7.6% for 1-20 hours, 10.8% to 13.6% for 21-39 hours), while the full-time (40 hours) and more than full-time (41-60 hours), categories added 5.9% and 9.0%, respectively. Both of the latter figures easily exceed the 5% standard for real change, and the shift in the 0 column nearly quadruples it.

Table 3.6 Hours Worked by Decade for males and females
3.6a: Males

	Hours Worked					
	0	1-20	21-39	40	41-60	61+
1970s	34.4%	3.2%	7.3%	27.9%	22.7%	4.6%
1980s	27.8%	4.3%	8.7%	26.0%	26.7%	6.4%
1990s	25.9%	4.6%	8.5%	22.6%	31.0%	7.2%

n = 15,799

3.6b: Females

	Hours Worked					
	0	1-20	21-39	40	41-60	61+
1970s	63.0%	6.2%	10.8%	14.5%	5.1%	0.5%
1980s	49.9%	7.2%	12.8%	18.1%	10.5%	1.5%
1990s	42.2%	7.6%	13.6%	20.4%	14.1%	2.1%

n = 20,769

The men shown in Table 3.6a, by contrast, decreased their full-time in-volvement by about 5% (27.9% to 22.6%), while flowing into more than full-time in such numbers that it is now the largest hours fraction (31.0%). Easily missed but too large to dismiss is the *drop* in American men not working at all (34.4% down to 25.9% in 0 hours worked). This cues up questions of age-grading first posed in the General Patterns section.[12]

Age

An overview to these questions is provided by the familiar age breakdown sepa-rating Tables 3.7a, b and c. Americans under 30 are clearly working more than they did a generation ago. The drop in non-workers (43.1% to 28.3%) is accompanied by rises in every other category *except* 40 hours per week. Table 3.7b covering mid-life workers shows an even steeper drop in non-workers (37.9% to 18.4%), and a steeper rise in the 41-60 hours share (17.7% to 29.5%). Americans 50 years old and older have also left the non-working category, but in considerably lesser numbers than in Tables 3.7a and b (in Table 3.7c, 0 hours drops from 66.5% to 60.1%).[13]

Table 3.7 Hours Worked by Decade for younger, middle-aged and older adults
3.7a: Age Less Than 30

	Hours Worked					
	0	1-20	21-39	40	41-60	61+
1970s	43.1%	6.0%	11.5%	24.2%	12.6%	2.5%
1980s	31.4%	7.9%	13.8%	22.6%	20.6%	3.8%
1990s	28.3%	9.4%	15.1%	20.8%	22.3%	4.0%

n = 8,355

3.7b: Age 30-49

	Hours Worked					
	0	1-20	21-39	40	41-60	61+
1970s	37.9%	5.3%	10.9%	25.0%	17.7%	3.3%
1980s	22.3%	5.9%	13.0%	29.2%	24.2%	5.4%
1990s	18.4%	5.7%	12.9%	27.7%	29.5%	5.8%

n = 14,489

3.7c: Age 50+

	Hours Worked					
	0	1-20	21-39	40	41-60	61+
1970s	66.5%	3.8%	6.3%	13.5%	8.5%	1.2%
1980s	64.5%	4.9%	7.3%	13.0%	8.7%	1.7%
1990s	60.1%	5.3%	7.5%	13.6%	10.8%	2.7%

n = 13,609

Internal shifts aside, a crude age grading is apparent across the tables in that mid-career adults are outworking younger adults, who, in turn, are outworking older adults. Age-grading aside, one suspects that the internal shifts by age are affected by sex, the other ascribed trait showing such strong trends in Table 3.6. This is precisely the sort of complication addressed by Modeling Trends in Chapter 8.

Education

Models built by social scientists and parents alike view school degrees as tickets to success. A sheepskin is "human capital" that can be exchanged for a better salary and a better job by its human bearer. But education is also a primary form of social involvement that—as has been argued above and will be documented below—is a veritable philosopher's stone for converting human capital into social capital.

Formal and parental theories are both mute, however, on just *how* school years get traded for success. The assumption seems to be that once a degree is awarded, it somehow functions as an ascribed trait opening up the doors of opportunity. The evidence here suggests that schooling actually controls how long and hard Americans push at the door.[14]

Table 3.8a shows no real change in the work involvement of Americans without a high school degree; about two-thirds continue to not work at all, and no hourly category changes by as much as 3%. Changes are readily apparent for the high school graduates in Table 3.8b. Nonworkers drop by over 10% (45.0% to 33.9% in the 0 hours column), and the numbers rise over 6% in the 41-60 hours column. College respondents already led the pack in work hours in the Seventies, then extended that lead by adding the largest fraction to the more-than-full time category by the Nineties (for 41-60 hours, the share went from 19.7% to 30.4%).[15]

Table 3.8 Hours Worked by Decade for levels of education
3.8a: Less Than High School

	Hours Worked					
	0	1-20	21-39	40	41-60	61+
1970s	66.2%	4.2%	6.5%	13.6%	1.2%	2.5%
1980s	64.7%	4.8%	8.0%	11.9%	1.9%	3.8%
1990s	63.5%	4.7%	8.0%	12.3%	2.2%	4.0%

n = 9,262

3.8b: High School

	Hours Worked					
	0	1-20	21-39	40	41-60	61+
1970s	45.0%	5.4%	10.1%	23.0%	13.8%	2.7%
1980s	35.9%	6.8%	12.7%	23.7%	17.2%	3.6%
1990s	33.9%	7.1%	12.4%	22.0%	20.3%	4.3%

n = 18,898

3.8c: College

	Hours Worked					
	0	1-20	21-39	40	41-60	61+
1970s	31.0%	5.0%	13.2%	27.9%	19.7%	3.2%
1980s	21.6%	5.4%	10.7%	27.8%	28.9%	5.7%
1990s	21.1%	5.7%	11.6%	25.4%	30.4%	5.7%

n = 8,299

The racing analogy may be apt, but it has two limits. First of all, the image of individuals racing harder and faster draws attention away from the conditions under which the race is run. Quite simply, education is the gatekeeper to the types of job "races" in which longer hours are both available and beneficial. Wall Streeters can work harder and expect more of a payoff, while Walmarters may work only up to the 35-hour limit of employment benefits that also keeps them out of the management track. Moreover, the Societal Trends just charted have occurred during a period of steepening social inequality in America. Chapter 9 will address how socioeconomic conditions surrounding the achievement race have impacted the accumulation of social capital. The second limitation concerns the image of the solitary runner. The analogy is apt insofar as the worker who puts in the laps can earn the ribbon of occupational success, but s/he does not do so alone. The workplace is a site of committees, conferences and water-cooler conversations—its very own source of *social* capital. It is the source of other kinds of social capital as well, as illustrated by Figure 3.1. It charts the number of times SCCBS respondents say they have "socialized with co-workers outside of work" in the past year. Note that the dots representing the mean amount of socializing rise with hours on the job. Americans working 1-20 hours averaged about 9 occasions, whereas 60+ hours workers nearly doubled that amount (9.5 vs. 16.7 co-worker occasions, respectively); the only exception to this accumulation of interaction with the accumulation of work time is the dip at 40 hours. This is only the most obvious of illustration of the compounding of social capital that is the subject of Chapter 7. It is also an obvious teaser for the mysteries of intimate interaction probed in Chapter 5.

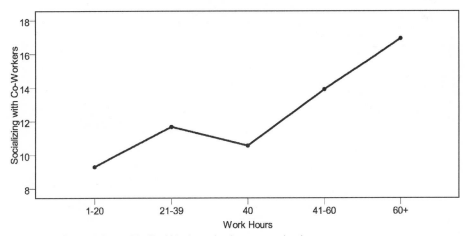

Figure 3.1 Socializing with Co-Workers by hours worked

ON THE "GREAT RECESSION"

In the LOOKING BACKWARD section that concluded Chapter 1, there is a full explanation of why the analytical spotlight is trained on the 1970-2000 period.

Given the economic plate-tectonics of the late 2000s, it is reasonable to wonder whether the trends in employment tracked here have been derailed in our seismically rocked society.

Two things. First, the successor volume to *Social Capital in America* will directly examine the employment evidence through 2010. Second, it is important to realize that the final three decades of the 20th century were rocked by four separate recessions. Even more to the point, in 1982 the unemployment rate topped out at 10.8%, well above the level of the so-called "Great Recession." Economic cycles do not necessarily uproot deeper, decade-by-decade shifts in social capital.

4

Family

Once the concept is introduced, there is an "of course" acknowledgement of family as a form of social capital. Clichés about the "building block of society" or the "cornerstone of civilization" made the family a natural nominee as a model component in Chapter 2. Equally clichéd is the observation that the American family is in decline. Pundits promoting the phrase "family values" almost always take that value to be falling. The public's level of concern about family breakdown is evident in the poll results summarized in Chapter 1, and in the anxious advice of Moms everywhere.

GENERAL PATTERNS

The national consensus on the state of American families dissolves into debate about just what a family *is*. Does gay marriage create a true "family" household? Can female—or male—headed households uphold traditional "family values"? Answers to such difficult and acrimonious questions transcend the scope of this book. The direct answers to be offered here concern the responses to two simple questions: 1) What is your current marital status, and 2) How many children, aged 17 or younger, live in your household? These questions give concrete form to the theoretical view in Chapter 2 that, "Family behaviors, including marriage and childbearing, remain the classic examples of investment in social capital."[1]

Sex

The combined answers to these two "simple questions" produce a finely textured profile of family in America. Despite the symmetrical assumption of traditional marriage—one man, one woman—there are substantial differences in family structure by sex. The columns in Table 4.1 are roughly arranged from lower to higher levels of family commitment, from left to right. So the folks at far left have made no formal investments at all in family life; they are people with neither marital nor parental commitments. Note that one out of five males (20.4%) has this family non-status compared to about one out of eight women (12.1%). The proportions shift back in the other direction for the second column, signifying respondents who were once married (now divorced, widowed or separated), and who have no resident children; this status is occupied by about one-sixth (16.2%) of all women compared to only about a tenth of all men (10.5%). The proportions of American men and women who have never married with at least one resident child are approximately balanced (7.6% and 8.3%). Although the numbers are relatively small, another sex difference appears among formerly married respondents living with children (column 4), for whom females outnumber males nearly two-to-one (7.1% vs. 3.7%). The currently married with no resident children (many of whom did raise kids) are closely matched by sex (30.0% vs. 28.7%), as is the far right column indicating adults currently married with resident children (27.7% vs. 27.6%).

Table 4.1 Sex and Family Status

	Family Status					
	Never married, no children (1)	Once married, no children (2)	Never married, w/children (3)	Once married, w/children (4)	Married, no children (5)	Married, w/children (6)
Males	20.4%	10.5%	7.6%	3.7%	30.0%	27.7%
Females	12.1%	16.2%	8.3%	7.1%	28.7%	27.6%

n = 29,000

Clearly, social capital as measured by family status represents a diverse portfolio in contemporary America. The most invested with the dual family commitments of marriage *and* parenting are just over a quarter of adults of both sexes. Moving left into the intermediary levels of family commitment, the continued sexual division of labor in child-rearing is apparent in the higher proportions of females in the formerly married with children and never married with children areas. A good part of the difference in column 2 is attributable to widowhood (about half of all women in this status are widows, compared to less than a quarter of men). At the far left are Americans with a score of zero in the marriage plus children equation, most of whom are male. Before over-interpreting this datum's meaning for commitment to the family as social capital, it is important to consider the action of life stage on family status.[2]

Age

As expected, the never married and childless status is dominated by young adults in Table 4.2. The first column is by far the fullest for Americans under 30 (40.4%). The only status that bears any comparison at all for young adults is in column 3, holding those who are never married with children (26.9%). Both of those columns shrink substantially in middle adulthood, evidence of the "action of life stage" referred to above. The dominant area for 30-49 year-old Americans is at far right for married with kids (49.3%). The passage to mature adulthood is marked by the expansion of column 5—married with no resident children—to a full 56.1% of Americans 50 and up. The only other status in the older row with double-figure percentages is once married, no children with about a quarter (26.7%) in column 2.[3]

Table 4.2 Age and Family Status

	Family Status					
	Never married, no children (1)	Once married, no children (2)	Never married, w/children (3)	Once married, w/children (4)	Married, no children (5)	Married, w/children (6)
< 30	40.4%	1.5%	26.9%	2.9%	10.2%	18.1%
30-49	12.8%	8.0%	4.5%	8.7%	16.8%	49.3%
50+	4.7%	26.7%	0.4%	3.5%	56.1%	8.6%

n = 28,349

The data-driven temptation is to view the columnar shifts as *entirely* a life-cycle progression from low, to high, to medium levels of family commitment. The reality of that progression is undeniable, but there are other processes potentially at work. Notably, fewer Americans than ever are getting married, and those who do are waiting longer in their lives; moreover, childbearing rates here are well below Baby Boomer levels. The implication is that Table 4.2 also bears the imprint of wider Societal Trends to be addressed in the next section.

Education

The most consistent General Pattern threading through all of these analyses is the effect of education upon social capital. There is no exception in Table 4.3. The relatively heavier deposit of college respondents at the bottom of the first column (18.7% vs. 12.3% for high school graduates and 11.4% for the less than high school respondents) echoes reservations concerning the intertwining of Societal Trends. After all, the trend toward more schooling will have concentrated college grads at younger, more single-prone years, a dual link of age and education to keep in mind in analyses to come. For all other statuses, education seems to be family-friendly. Collegiate respondents are about half as likely to be in columns 2 (once married without a child present) and 3 (never married with a child present), and a bit less likely to be in column 4 (once married with a child present) than are the less than high school set; high school grads are between the educational extremes in each of these columns. The married with no children status shows little difference by schooling (all between 26.3% and 30.2%), but the double commitment, married with children area is larger at each higher educational level (23.0% for less than high school, 25.9% for high school, 29.4% for college). Clearly, the educational effect operates even for that most intimate of social structures—the family.[4]

Table 4.3 Education and Family Status

| | Family Status | | | | | |
	Never married, no children (1)	Once married, no children (2)	Never married, w/children (3)	Once married, w/children (4)	Married, no children (5)	Married, w/children (6)
Less than high school	11.4%	20.1%	12.4%	6.8%	26.3%	23.0%
High school	12.3%	14.4%	11.1%	6.1%	30.2%	25.9%
College	18.7%	11.8%	5.7%	5.0%	29.5%	29.4%

$n = 28,697$

Race

The racial comparison produces several salient contrasts in family status, especially in the middle columns. Starting with (5), white Americans are more than twice as likely to be married without children than black Americans (34.3% to 16.5%). Those percentages switch under once married with children (4) and never married with children (3) in which black respondents predominate by 5% and 14.2%, respectively.

Table 4.4 Race and Family Status

| | Family Status | | | | | |
	Never married, no children (1)	Once married, no children (2)	Never married, w/children (3)	Once married, w/children (4)	Married, no children (5)	Married, w/children (6)
White	15.3%	14.2%	4.6%	4.7%	34.3%	27.0%
Black	16.4%	15.3%	18.8%	9.7%	16.5%	23.2%

$n = 23,968$

SOCIETAL TRENDS

The concern of pundits and the public alike about the state of the American family is not unfounded. Suggestive evidence of changing family structures included in the General Patterns discussion takes concrete form in the present section.

Sex

To accommodate the shift in emphasis to social change in the present section, the definition of family statuses will be altered slightly. Here, the "with children" categories will not be limited to those having offspring under the age of 17 in the household. That tighter definition made sense in the previous section to highlight the current composition of American families. In the tables below, having a child of any age will be considered a lifetime commitment, which is a truism many older parents ruefully acknowledge.

Table 4.5 Family Status by Decade for males and females
4.5a: Males

	Family Status					
	Never married, no children (1)	Once married, no children (2)	Never married, w/children (3)	Once married, w/children (4)	Married, no children (5)	Married, w/children (6)
1970s	16.0%	2.7%	0.8%	8.5%	10.7%	61.4%
1980s	20.9%	2.9%	1.4%	12.3%	8.7%	53.8%
1990s	22.1%	4.0%	2.7%	15.9%	7.9%	47.3%

$n = 16,657$

4.5b: Females

	Family Status					
	Never married, no children (1)	Once married, no children (2)	Never married, w/children (3)	Once married, w/children (4)	Married, no children (5)	Married, w/children (6)
1970s	9.2%	3.7%	1.6%	21.0%	8.5%	55.9%
1980s	12.0%	4.6%	3.0%	28.1%	7.5%	44.8%
1990s	12.8%	4.5%	6.0%	30.0%	6.3%	40.5%

$n = 21,322$

Since the married-with-children status is the touchstone for discussions of the "traditional" American family, let us begin by unpacking trends in the right-hand columns. In the decade of the Seventies, 6 out of every 10 males in Table 4.5a had this dual investment in family capital (61.4%); by the Nineties, the double commitment had slipped to less than half of men (47.3%). As one would expect given the symmetry of this status, American women also sold off traditional family capital in this category (55.9% down to 40.5% in Table 4.5b). For both sexes, changes in the married without children column dropped only a few percentage points over the period. The once married with no children and never married with children (columns 2 and 3, respectively) remained rare family statuses over this period, but did increase a bit. Both sexes expanded their positions in the once married with children status, males in column 4 nearly doubling to 15.9% (from 8.5%), and females growing from 21.0% in the Seventies to 30.0% in the Nineties. The no family commitment columns on the left were also sites of some change. Never-married, childless males increased to easily exceed our 5% standard for significant change (16.0% to 22.1%) and the female change followed suit but topped out at the lower percentage of 12.8% (from 9.2%).

Despite a few diverting sex differences and a big knot of numbers, the overall trends in family commitment are simplicity itself: male and female Americans are both divesting the higher levels of family commitment in the right-hand columns of Table 4.5 in favor of the more liquid assets of family capital on the Table's left.[6]

Age

Table 4.6 is a return to the familiar puzzle of life-cycle versus social change that also contains some real answers. While everyday experience and sophisticated cohort studies reveal higher family investment in middle adulthood regardless of decade, decade clearly matters, too.

Table 4.6 Family Status by Decade for younger, middle-aged and older adults

4.6a: Less than 30

	Family Status					
	Never married, no children	Once married, no children	Never married, w/children	Once married, w/children	Married, no children	Married, w/children
	(1)	(2)	(3)	(4)	(5)	(6)
1970s	35.2%	1.9%	3.4%	5.2%	17.1%	37.1%
1980s	43.2%	2.4%	5.7%	7.0%	14.9%	26.8%
1990s	49.1%	1.9%	11.7%	5.4%	11.8%	20.1%

n = 8,642

4.6b: 30-49

	Family Status					
	Never married, no children	Once married, no children	Never married, w/children	Once married, w/children	Married, no children	Married, w/children
	(1)	(2)	(3)	(4)	(5)	(6)
1970s	4.5%	1.6%	0.9%	12.5%	5.6%	75.0%
1980s	9.4%	3.2%	2.2%	19.0%	6.9%	59.2%
1990s	12.5%	4.7%	4.5%	20.7%	7.7%	49.9%

n = 15,031

4.6c: 50+

	Family Status					
	Never married, no children	Once married, no children	Never married, w/children	Once married, w/children	Married, no children	Married, w/children
	(1)	(2)	(3)	(4)	(5)	(6)
1970s	4.4%	5.5%	0.1%	24.3%	8.1%	57.6%
1980s	4.8%	5.4%	0.3%	32.5%	4.9%	52.1%
1990s	5.0%	4.9%	0.7%	37.9%	3.6%	47.9%

n = 14,184

In the left-hand column of Table 4.6a is a steady march into the unmarried-and-childless status from 35.2% of young Americans in the Seventies to 49.1% in the Nineties. Most of them appear to have stepped out of the married with children (37.1% down to 20.1%) and married without children (17.1% down to 11.8%) categories at right.

Middle adulthood, of course, is the well-known staging site of family capitalization. A cursory comparison of the rows in Tables 4.6a and 4.6b shows 30-49 year olds to be much more built up in the married with children status (49.9% versus 20.1% for Americans under 30 in the 1990s), while young adults stack up higher in the never married without children end (49.1% versus 12.5% for Americans 30-49 in the 1990s.) This tabular format allows us to look past life-cycle effects to looming Societal Trends by simply inspecting the columns. "Loom" appears to be the proper disquieting word. The double investment of marriage plus children de-capitalized from a full three-quarters of middle-aged adults in the Seventies to just under half in the Nineties (49.9%). The married and childless status made a marginal gain (5.6% to 7.7%), but most of the jumps in the 30-49 portfolio appear at the low end of family capitalization.

In general, older Americans manifest more modest decade-to-decade changes in family status. Both high-end investments in marriage declined (married with children down from 57.6% to 47.9%, married without children down from 8.1% to 3.6%). The largest spike is in the once married with children column, which gained well over twice the rule of thumb percentage for a significant shift (24.3% to 37.9%, over a 10% change). This suggests a pretty straightforward redistribution of older Americans due to marital dissolution.

Beyond suggestion in the zone of documented fact is this conclusion: at all ages, American family structures have clearly been decapitalizing over the last three decades.[7]

Education

We now also know for a fact (or, a General Pattern) that higher levels of education are generally associated with higher levels of family capital. The exception is the relatively greater proportion of college-educated adults who are neither married nor parents, which was speculated to be the result of college education being concentrated at younger ages. Untangling this complex conundrum must await the model building of Chapters 7 and 8.

Of immediate relevance, though, is a factual frame for Societal Trends involving education. It is important to remember that American adults are flowing fast to higher levels of schooling. But there are important flows *inside* educational categories as well. A little less than six in ten American adults without high school degrees were married with children in the 1970s (58.1% in Table 4.7a), which dropped nearly twenty percentage points by the 1990s (to 39.1%). Table 4.7b shows a steep decline in "traditional" family capital among high school graduates; 59.7% of the latter were married with children at the top of the column, compared to only 43.6% at the bottom—a slide of about 16%. The slide for college respondents is not quite as steep, but is evident nevertheless in the 55.1% to 45.8% drop in the married with children column of Table 4.7c.

Table 4.7 Family Status by Decade for levels of education
4.7a: Less than high school

	Family Status					
	Never married, no children (1)	Once married, no children (2)	Never married, w/children (3)	Once married, w/children (4)	Married, no children (5)	Married, w/children (6)
1970s	7.0%	3.9%	1.7%	22.2%	7.1%	58.1%
1980s	9.4%	4.6%	3.3%	33.0%	4.6%	45.1%
1990s	11.1%	4.6%	7.0%	34.7%	3.5%	39.1%

n = 9,789

4.7b: High School

	Family Status					
	Never married, no children (1)	Once married, no children (2)	Never married, w/children (3)	Once married, w/children (4)	Married, no children (5)	Married, w/children (6)
1970s	14.3%	2.6%	1.1%	12.2%	10.0%	59.7%
1980s	16.2%	3.4%	2.4%	18.7%	7.9%	51.5%
1990s	16.7%	3.8%	5.1%	24.7%	6.2%	43.6%

n = 19,563

4.7c: College

	Family Status					
	Never married, no children (1)	Once married, no children (2)	Never married, w/children (3)	Once married, w/children (4)	Married, no children (5)	Married, w/children (6)
1970s	18.4%	3.7%	0.4%	8.7%	13.8%	55.1%
1980s	22.9%	4.1%	1.0%	13.1%	12.7%	46.1%
1990s	20.5%	4.7%	2.0%	16.3%	10.6%	45.8%

n = 8,505

Because of the simple logic of percentages, fewer full, "traditional" families means more Americans with lesser levels of capital commitment. So: all four not-married columns grow for all educational levels in Table 4.7. Especially notable is the surge in once married with children respondents who swell about 12% in the less than high school and high school subtables (22.2% to 34.7%, and 12.2% to 24.7% respectively), and just under 8% among college respondents (8.7% to 16.3%). Please also note that the never married with no children column at left shows very little increase for all educational levels. The main differences are *across* educational levels, with more educated respondents more likely to have made no family investments regardless of decade.[8]

The decline of the American family over the last generation is a cliché of our popular culture. Indeed, the surveys reviewed in Chapter 1 suggest a widening public view that family breakdown is de-establishing American society itself. There is no shortage of experts lending credence to this sense of alarm. In the late 1990s book entitled *The State of Americans*, a team of social scientists offered this statement as a preface to their own data:

> There is a growing body of scientific evidence that the process of making human beings human is breaking down in American society... and the indications from the evidence are that these trends will be continuing at an increasing rate. The causes of this breakdown are, of course, manifold, but they all converge in their disruptive impact on the one institution that bears primary responsibility for socialization in our society—the American family.[9]

The present analysis leans less on apocalyptic pronouncements and more on capital accounting. And that accounting has surely shown an accumulation of debits for the traditional married with children family status. The overriding question is what this means for the whole pattern of social capital in America, a question this text is not yet prepared to answer. Even on the smaller balance sheet of family itself, there are factors here that transcend simple, scary stories of societal breakdown.

In the first place, the "decline" of extant marriages appears to have stopped. The divorce rate did increase during the 1970s, but has not changed significantly since 1980; this fits with the generally larger increases in the "once married" columns from 1970s to 1980s than for 1980s to 1990s in the Tables above.[10] A second qualifying demographic fact concerns *when* Americans get married: "Between 1960 and 1997, the median age at first marriage rose from 22.8 to 26.8 years for men and from 20.3 to 25.0 years for women."[11] This bears directly on the mounting numbers in the left-hand column of respondents under 30 in Table 4.6, and it strongly suggests that the end of traditional marriage is not nigh. According to *All Our Families*, another recent book penned by another panel of family experts, "...about 90% of Americans are still likely to marry at some point in their lifetime, and virtually all who do either have, or at least want to have, children."[12] Several national surveys of young Americans find that marriage and children are among their most cherished life objectives, and that these "family values" (literally) are *not* slipping.[13] There has been some serious decapitalization, but little prospect of an across-the-board crash of family social capital.

5

Social Networks

In the vast emptiness of America,
loneliness was from the beginning
an enemy to be conquered; nowhere was
war waged on it more determinedly...
— *Theodore Zeldin,*
An Intimate History of Humanity

In many respects, social networks are the most private form of social capital. Interpersonal relations with friends, relatives, and neighbors are both less official and more voluntary than other kinds of association. Even the spousal relationship—the usual referent of the term "intimate"—has dual status in the official, public institution of marriage; job statistics are matters of public record on the evening news; even though they are "voluntary" associations, PTAs and bowling teams involve formal commitments and membership lists. By contrast, personal relationships are an entirely personal matter. As such, they are the most *buried* of all forms of social capital *treasure*, amassed entirely out of public view, which is where they seem to belong.

It is only over the recent period covered by Social Trends that sociologists have unearthed social networks in any systematic way. That excavation has made two things perfectly clear. First, social networks are extremely valuable to me and to you as individuals. They help us to find jobs, to make life decisions, and to stay happy and healthy. Second, social networks are extremely valuable to society. A major—and enormously persuasive—segment of *Bowling Alone* is devoted to scholarly evidence that social structures like networks are the lifeblood of economic and educational institutions, of communities, and even of American democracy itself.[1]

Why use the term "network" to refer to the everyday reality of social relations? Because for each of us they form a complex pattern. Some of your friends are friends of each other; some are not. All of your cousins are interconnected on the family tree, but not all are invited to the Friday night poker game with your neighbors (and only a few of *them* are invited.) The point is that each set of relationships built up by an individual is a distinctive pattern of cross-cutting social links—quite like a net. Yours is referred to as an "egocentric network" due to this distinctiveness, and you really have not thought about mine. That is the immediate point. We are all so busy tending networks in our personal lives that it is hard to know—or even have time to think about—General Patterns.

GENERAL PATTERNS

The opening quote suggests that Americans are particularly active people in building and maintaining social networks. An interesting datum in this regard comes from the World Values Study encompassing over 50 societies. One of the survey questions was, "How important are friends in your life?" 69.4% of Americans responded that friendship is "very important," which placed U.S. society near the very top of the list.[2] This justifies starting the analysis of social networks by looking at friends.

Sex

The SCCBS 2000 dataset provides a direct count through the question, "About how many CLOSE FRIENDS do you have these days?" Table 5.1 shows a rough comparability among American males and females. However, the far right column reveals the fact that males are about 5% more likely than females (43.5% to 38.4%) to be in the upper category of 6 or more close friends.[3]

Table 5.1 Sex and Close Friends

	No. of Close Friends		
	0-2	3-5	6-10
Male	22.2%	34.3%	43.5%
Female	22.7%	38.9%	38.4%

n = 29,103

Table 5.2 focuses on relatives, but it is not a direct count of active relationships. The item is "How many times in the past 12 months have you visited relatives or had them visit you?" Measuring social contact is not the same as measuring social content, but it still reflects activity and commitment in an important zone of the social network. A real sex difference emerges here. Note that just over half of males are in the low category of kin visiting (51.4% visit monthly or less) compared to 44.7% for females. This significant difference is reproduced at the high end (more than three times a month) in the opposite direction (33.9% for females exceeds 26.5% for males). American women simply interact with their relatives more often than do American men.[4]

Table 5.2 Sex and Kin Visiting

	Visiting Relatives (Frequency in Past Year)		
	0-12	13-36	37-53
Male	51.4%	22.2%	26.5%
Female	44.7%	21.4%	33.9%

n = 28,611

The final sector of the social network to be spotlighted is neighboring. As the -ing would imply, this is again a measure of social contact: "About how often do you talk to or visit with your immediate neighbors?" Table 5.3 breaks down contact frequency into: never up to once a month, several times a month, several times a week, and just about every day. The close numerical match of all columns signifies no significant (i.e., 5%) sex differences in neighboring.[5] The general American gender pattern appears to be more close friendship among males, more visiting with relatives among females, and sex-similar interaction with neighbors.

Table 5.3 Sex and Neighbor Interaction

	Neighbor Interaction			
	never-once a month	several times a month	several times a week	daily
Male	26.7%	18.6%	31.9%	22.8%
Female	28.2%	18.1%	30.6%	23.1%

n = 29,026

Age

In the previous two chapters, there were cultural expectations brought to the age data on social capital. Known features of life stages in the U.S. led to the presumption of greatest work and family involvement in the middle years, and the data largely supported that presumption. Since private networks operate below our public radar, there is no such expectation here.

Nevertheless, Table 5.4 yields a clear, robust finding: older Americans have, on average, more friends. Notice that the top two rows match pretty closely, indicating no real differences (as great as 5%) between young and middle-aged adults. Over the age of 50, though, the low (0-2) proportion of close friends dives to its lowest point (19.1%), and the top category (6+ close friends) tops out at 47.7%, well above both other ages.[6]

Table 5.4 Age and Close Friends

	No. of Close Friends		
	0-2	3-5	6-10
< 30	22.3%	38.4%	39.3%
30-49	25.1%	39.3%	35.7%
50+	19.1%	33.2%	47.7%

n = 28,379

Kin visiting patterns do also show some age variation. In Table 5.5, oldsters are exactly 5% more likely to be with relatives monthly or less than are youngsters; this difference approximately switches at the high end of kin visiting (28.5% for 50+, 33.2% for < 30). There is no definitive explanation available for this finding, but two obvious candidates: 1. mature adults will have lost more relatives, to, well, too much maturity and, 2. they appear to be busier with their friends.[7]

Table 5.5 Age and Kin Visiting

	Visiting Relatives (Frequency in Past Year)		
	0-12	13-36	37-53
< 30	45.6%	21.2%	33.2%
30-49	46.2%	23.2%	30.6%
50+	50.6%	20.9%	28.5%

n = 27,927

A robust pattern does assert itself for neighboring. Note in Table 5.6 that the never to once a month percentage drops down the left column, and that the reverse happens in the daily neighboring column at right. At the extremes, older adults are 16.2% less likely to neighbor a little and 9.6% more likely to neighbor a lot than are younger adults; middle-aged adults neighbor in the middle.[8]

Table 5.6 Age and Neighbor Interaction

	Neighbor Interaction			
	never-once a month	several times a month	several times a week	daily
< 30	37.9%	18.6%	25.3%	18.1%
30-49	26.6%	19.7%	32.5%	21.1%
50+	21.7%	16.8%	33.8%	27.7%

n = 28,290

Education

Although cultural expectations are absent here, too, the weight of previous data bears down on education. Its ponderous effects on other kinds of social capital could lead social networks either way. Is education an open account for all forms of social capital? Or does heavy investment in work and family squeeze out social networks?

The first answer to the later question is "no" in Table 5.7. College respondents are much less likely to be at the lowest level of close friends (18.2% compared to 34.1%), and 5.5% more likely to be at the highest friendship level than less than high school respondents; as usual, high school respondents are in between.[9]

The clarity of the answer to the two questions posed above sharpens further in Table 5.8. More than six of ten (61.7%) of the top row are at the very lowest level of family visiting, a fraction that drops to about less than half in the middle (47.7%) and even lower in the bottom row (45.3%). High school (32.8%) and college (30.5%) respondents are both substantially more likely to be high visitors with relatives than are those in the less than high school row (23.6%). More education means friends *and* more time with kin.[10]

Table 5.7 Education and Close Friends

	No. of Close Friends		
	0-2	3-5	6-10
Less than high school	34.1%	28.7%	37.2%
High school	26.7%	34.9%	38.4%
College	18.2%	39.2%	42.7%

n = 28,774

Table 5.8 Education and Kin Visiting

	Visiting Relatives (Frequency in Past Year)		
	0-12	13-36	37-53
Less than high school	61.7%	14.7%	23.6%
High school	47.7%	19.6%	32.8%
College	45.3%	24.2%	30.5%

n = 28,301

Table 5.9 completes the network trifecta. Although no significant differences appear at the top end of daily neighboring (all between 22.3% and 25.2%), an educational gap does open elsewhere. One in three (33.2%) of college respondents neighbor several times a week compared to only about one in five (21.7%) less than high school respondents. The pro-neighboring education effect is further confirmed in the dropping percentages down the "never - once per month" column.[11]

Table 5.9 Education and Neighbor Interaction

	Neighbor Interaction			
	never-once a month	several times a month	several times a week	daily
Less than high school	39.1%	14.0%	21.7%	25.2%
High school	28.7%	17.0%	30.9%	23.4%
College	24.7%	19.8%	33.2%	22.3%

n = 28,678

In the terms of the chapter opening, more educated Americans wage war "more determinedly" against loneliness than do less educated Americans by fortifying their social networks with friends, relatives and neighbors alike.

Race

The series of race tables yields social network differences every bit as substantial as those for education. Of course, a straightforward reason for this is that substantial education differences overlay race. This is a complication to be unraveled in Chapter 9, but the data here are clear and consistent: black respondents in the SCCBS report less interpersonal interaction. They are over 20% more likely to have low levels of close friends (39.2% vs. 17.8%),[12] about 8% more likely to be low in kin visiting frequency (52.3% vs. 44.4%),[13] and over 12% more likely to be infrequent neighbor interactors (35.6% to 23.4%) than white respondents.[14] Social networks in America certainly do differ by race.

Table 5.10 Race and Close Friends

	No. of Close Friends		
	0-2	3-5	6-10
White	17.8%	37.3%	44.9%
Black	39.2%	35.2%	25.6%

n = 24,026

Table 5.11 Race and Kin Visiting

	Visiting Relatives (Frequency in Past Year)		
	0-12	13-36	37-53
White	44.4%	23.5%	32.1%
Black	52.3%	18.9%	28.8%

n = 23,639

Table 5.12 Race and Neighbor Interaction

	Neighbor Interaction			
	never-once a month	several times a month	several times a week	daily
White	23.4%	19.5%	33.5%	23.6%
Black	35.6%	14.1%	25.1%	25.2%

n = 23,963

SOCIETAL TRENDS

As we approach Chapter 7, it becomes increasingly difficult to think of social capital in its separate accounts. Knowing that work is up and that family structure is down over time makes it hard to conceive of social networks as unchanged. That is the reason, of course, for building a Model of Social Capital that explicitly examines transactions *across* these accounts as a template for viewing capital flows. But even though they are only part of the overall portfolio, changes in social networks could certainly change the overall value of social capital in America.

The General Social Survey offers no comprehensive archive of personal relationships over time in the U.S.—in fact, no such archive exists.[15] However, the GSS does offer trend data on frequency of social contact for the same three network relations surveyed in General Patterns: friends, relatives, and neighbors.

Sex

Table 5.13 compiles responses to this question: "How often do you spend a social evening with friends who live outside the neighborhood?" It is important to observe up front that this particular wording will tend to elicit very particular kinds of interaction. "Spend a social evening" sounds like a special occasion rather than picking up a buddy to go to the gym. Nevertheless, it would seem to be a valid reflector of friendship, and it also parallels the wording for the other two network relations. At the high end of friend socializing ("several times a week" to "almost daily"), there is precious little evidence of change among American males in Table 5.13a; 22.7% interacted at this level in the 1970s compared to 24.7% in the 1990s, a "shift" of only 2%. Similar non-changes appear in the low ("never" to "several times a year") and medium ("once" to "several times a month") columns. Table 5.13b shows only one significant shift: females in the Nineties are 5.1% less likely to be at the low level of interaction than they were in the Seventies (34.9% versus 40.0%, respectively). So: friendship socializing seems to have changed not at all among American males and, if anything, seems to have gotten less infrequent among American females.[16]

Table 5.13 Friend Socializing by Decade for males and females

5.13a: Males

	never-several times a year	once to several times a month	several times a week-almost daily
1970s	36.7%	40.6%	22.7%
1980s	35.6%	41.4%	23.0%
1990s	33.9%	41.4%	24.7%

n = 10,108

5.13b: Females

	never-several times a year	once to several times a month	several times a week-almost daily
1970s	40.0%	39.5%	20.6%
1980s	36.5%	42.8%	20.7%
1990s	34.9%	43.3%	21.8%

n = 13,125

For the "How often do you spend a social evening with relatives" question, another sex-specific change is apparent. The slippage at the high level in Table

5.14a stops just short of our 5% standard of change (it drops 4.9%), but no column in Table 5.14b budges by much more than 2%.

American men have become (marginally) less likely to visit kin at a high level, and American women have kept their Seventies pattern intact.[17]

Table 5.14 Kin Socializing by Decade for males and females

5.14a: Males

	never-several times a year	once to several times a month	several times a week-almost daily
1970s	29.9%	35.4%	34.7%
1980s	34.1%	34.1%	31.8%
1990s	34.1%	36.1%	29.8%

n = 10,114

5.14b: Females

	never-several times a year	once to several times a month	several times a week-almost daily
1970s	27.0%	33.3%	39.7%
1980s	28.8%	34.0%	37.2%
1990s	27.0%	34.8%	38.2%

n = 13,134

Sweeping changes do appear in Tables 5.15. The frequency with which people "…spend a social evening with someone in your neighborhood" is clearly down. High frequency of this kind of neighboring dropped from 29.0% to 22.6% in Table 5.15a, a change of 6.4%; the low end rose from 43.5% to 50.1%, a net of nearly 7%. The shifts in Table 5.15b are at least as strong: high neighboring dropped 7.6% (29.2% to 21.6%), and low neighboring rose 9% (43.9% to 52.9%). American males and females clearly spend nights out with neighbors less than they used to.[18]

Table 5.15 Neighbor Socializing by Decade for males and females

5.15a: Males

	never-several times a year	once to several times a month	several times a week-almost daily
1970s	43.5%	27.5%	29.0%
1980s	47.5%	27.5%	25.0%
1990s	50.1%	27.2%	22.6%

n = 10,095

5.15b: Females

	Never-several times a year	once to several times a month	several times a week-almost daily
1970s	43.9%	26.9%	29.2%
1980s	48.5%	26.4%	25.1%
1990s	52.9%	25.5%	21.6%

n = 13,126

Age

On average, young American adults are more friend-friendly than they were a generation ago. This conclusion is based on the right-hand column of Table 5.16a, showing a 5.3% surge in high levels of friendship interaction from the 1970s (36.0%) to the 1990s (41.3%). No column approaches this standard of change in Table 5.16b, thus indicating unchanged patterns of friendship visiting among middle-age adults. The older adults shown in Table 5.16c, however, got out more with friends as shown by the drop in the low column from 52.1% to 46.1% (a net of 6%). Younger and older Americans socialize with friends *more* than before, and middle-aged Americans socialize no less.[19]

Table 5.16 Friend Socializing by Decade for young, middle-aged and older adults
5.16a: Less than 30

	never-several times a year	once to several times a month	several times a week-almost daily
1970s	19.9%	44.1%	36.0%
1980s	18.6%	45.5%	36.0%
1990s	16.2%	42.5%	41.3%

n = 5,295

5.16b: 30-49

	never-several times a year	once to several times a month	several times a week-almost daily
1970s	37.4%	43.4%	19.2%
1980s	32.5%	46.9%	20.7%
1990s	33.0%	45.5%	21.5%

n = 9,201

5.16c: 50+

	never-several times a year	once to several times a month	several times a week-almost daily
1970s	52.1%	34.1%	13.8%
1980s	50.8%	35.6%	13.6%
1990s	46.1%	38.7%	15.2%

n = 8,663

Tables 5.17a, 5.17b and 5.17c fail to show such any age-specific pattern of change. In fact, they fail to show any real change at all; no column alters by as much as 4%. "Social evenings with relatives" in the last decade were pretty much the same as they were in the Seventies for Americans of all ages.[20]

Table 5.17 Kin Socializing by Decade for young, middle-aged and older adults

5.17a: Less than 30

	never-several times a year	once to several times a month	several times a week-almost daily
1970s	21.8%	32.4%	45.7%
1980s	24.7%	33.5%	41.7%
1990s	23.3%	34.1%	42.6%

n = 5,293

5.17b: 30-49

	never-several times a year	once to several times a month	several times a week-almost daily
1970s	30.6%	36.3%	33.1%
1980s	32.0%	36.5%	31.5%
1990s	30.9%	36.8%	32.4%

n = 9,205

5.17c: 50+

	never-several times a year	once to several times a month	several times a week-almost daily
1970s	30.5%	33.4%	36.1%
1980s	34.1%	32.0%	33.9%
1990s	32.6%	34.3%	33.2%

n = 8,677

Another uniform pattern can be found in Table 5.18: neighboring is down across all ages. The young adults in Table 5.18a are nearly 10% more likely to neighbor at a low rate (34.3% versus 44.1%), and 7% less likely to neighbor at a high rate (38.9% versus 31.9%) than they used to be. The comparable columns in Tables 5.18b and 5.18c show similar shifts, and all are beyond our 5% standard for change.[21]

Table 5.18 Neighbor Socializing by Decade for young, middle-aged and older adults

5.18a: Less than 30

	never-several times a year	once to several times a month	several times a week-almost daily
1970s	34.3%	26.7%	38.9%
1980s	37.7%	27.2%	35.1%
1990s	44.1%	24.0%	31.9%

n = 5,293

5.18b: 30-49

	never-several times a year	once to several times a month	several times a week-almost daily
1970s	46.1%	29.6%	24.3%
1980s	50.1%	29.9%	20.1%
1990s	53.5%	28.6%	17.9%

n = 9,188

5.18c: 50+

	never-several times a year	once to several times a month	several times a week-almost daily
1970s	47.9%	25.2%	26.9%
1980s	52.7%	23.9%	23.4%
1990s	53.6%	24.6%	21.8%

n = 8,668

To sum up trends by degree of change, then, kin visiting stayed rock-solid regardless of age, friend visiting built up among the young and old, and neighboring eroded across all American age groups.

Education

Until the last decade, just about half of all Americans without a high school diploma rarely went out with friends at all; this is reflected in the 1970s/49.9% and 1980s/50.0% figures in the low column of Table 5.19a, which then drops almost 5% by the 1990s (to 45.2%). High school and college-educated respondents were more socially active with their friends to begin with, and their overall patterns of interaction did not change detectably anywhere in Tables 5.19b or 5.19c.[22]

Table 5.19 Friend Socializing by Decade for adults with less than a high school education, a high school diploma, or college

5.19a: Less than high school

	never-several times a year	once to several times a month	several times a week-almost daily
1970s	49.9%	32.0%	18.1%
1980s	50.0%	30.8%	19.3%
1990s	45.2%	31.8%	23.0%

n = 5,760

5.19b: High school

	never-several times a year	once to several times a month	several times a week-almost daily
1970s	33.9%	42.2%	24.0%
1980s	33.1%	44.1%	22.8%
1990s	34.0%	42.3%	23.6%

n = 6,694

5.19c: College

	never-several times a year	once to several times a month	several times a week-almost daily
1970s	28.2%	50.4%	21.4%
1980s	26.5%	51.7%	21.7%
1990s	29.2%	48.9%	22.9%

n = 5,369

Thus far the most stable segment of American social networks has been kin visiting. Maintaining this pattern, Tables 5.20a, b and c each show no columnar shifts at all that meet our 5% sustained change standard.[23]

Table 5.20 Kin Socializing by Decade for adults with less than a high school education, a high school diploma, or college

5.20a: Less than high school

	never-several times a year	once to several times a month	several times a week-almost daily
1970s	25.5%	31.0%	43.5%
1980s	31.6%	28.1%	40.3%
1990s	30.0%	29.8%	40.3%

n = 5,771

5.20b: High school

	never-several times a year	once to several times a month	several times a week-almost daily
1970s	27.4%	35.4%	37.2%
1980s	28.0%	35.6%	36.3%
1990s	27.3%	35.7%	37.0%

n = 12,059

5.20c: College

	never-several times a year	once to several times a month	several times a week-almost daily
1970s	36.8%	37.8%	25.4%
1980s	38.0%	37.2%	24.9%
1990s	34.9%	38.0%	27.1%

n = 5,372

Thus far the least stable segment of American social networks has been neighboring, an instability that holds for the separate levels of education in Table 5.21. Low neighbor interaction rises 6% among less than high school respondents (45.6% to 51.4%). For high school and college respondents, the numbers in the low column rise even more (8.6% and 9.8%, respectively), and the numbers in the high neighboring column drop off significantly as well (down 5.7% and 8.3%, respectively).[24]

Table 5.21 Neighbor Socializing by Decade for adults with less than a high school education, a high school diploma, or college

5.21a: Less than high school

	never-several times a year	once to several times a month	several times a week-almost daily
1970s	45.6%	22.4%	32.1%
1980s	48.9%	20.1%	30.9%
1990s	51.4%	19.6%	29.0%

n = 5,762

5.21b: High school

	never-several times a year	once to several times a month	several times a week-almost daily
1970s	43.1%	28.9%	28.1%
1980s	47.6%	28.0%	24.4%
1990s	51.7%	25.9%	22.4%

n = 12,049

5.21c: College

	never-several times a year	once to several times a month	several times a week-almost daily
1970s	42.1%	32.2%	25.7%
1980s	48.2%	32.6%	19.2%
1990s	51.9%	30.7%	17.4%

n = 5,366

It is worth repeating the substantive point that our Social Trends have not been traced using formal counts of the friends, relatives and neighbors of all Americans. What we have here are serviceable—but indirect—measures of social network contact extending over three decades. As was argued in the WORK chapter, time spent in an activity is a measure of social commitment, and as was argued in the introduction to this chapter, commitment to social networks is investment in an important social capital account. In these terms, relatives are in long-term equilibrium, friends show signs of being bullish, and neighbors are a sustained bear market.

6

Voluntary Association

Do people really bowl *alone*?

  As a course exercise, I recently dispatched two classes of undergraduates to local bowling alleys. Armed with a simple survey, they were directed to approach an assortment of patrons over assorted days and nights. The survey was small (n = 79), selective (it was all conducted in the western suburbs of Philadelphia), and not supported by scientific sampling methods. Nevertheless, a breakdown of its data is instructive for the present exercise:

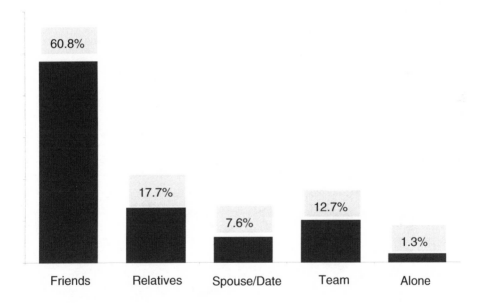

Figure 6.1 With whom do Americans bowl?

  A careful inspection of Figure 6.1 reveals that some people do, indeed, bowl alone. It takes careful inspection, though, because they are the shortest bar in the array; only 2 of the 79 (1.3%) bowlers were at the alleys by themselves. The number of team bowlers is only slighter larger (5), but would certainly be much larger if my students had deliberately surveyed on team nights. Over 90% of the bowlers had social network company—friends, relatives, spouses or dates. This is a not-so-subtle reminder that the forms of social capital are many and varied. Just counting "tea-mers" or "aloners" would have completely missed the most fundamental form of bowling association—precisely because it is not formally associational. The findings of this chapter (and the preceding three) require the structural guidance of the model of social capital upcoming in Chapter 7 to avoid such fundamental mistakes.

The summer survey yielded one other notable datum: about two-thirds of the bowlers were males. My mental picture of bowling in the last generation involves mostly guys, lots of beer, and a distinct "boys night out" mentality. Perhaps the male predominance in this generation carries vestiges of that, but the mental picture seems cracked and dated. The very notion of hard-working males stepping out together while homemaking wives remain home is more than a hopeless anachronism. It is another object lesson in the dangers of focusing on one form of social capital without taking account of the prodigious changes in family structures, career patterns and interpersonal expectations that now make guys in satin team jackets just seem silly.

GENERAL PATTERNS

It is time to look past intellectual caution flags at the actual stock of what is, for both Tocqueville and Putnam, the most precious form of social capital: voluntary association. A serviceable starting point is provided by the World Values Survey. Figure 6.2 presents an international comparison for overall membership rates across nine different forms of association (church, sports, arts/education, union, [political] party, environment, professional, charity and other):

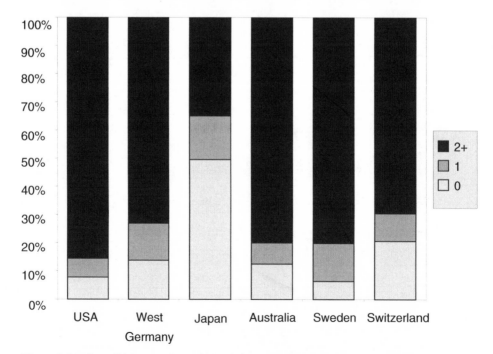

Figure 6.2 Index of Voluntary Association for six societies from the World Values Survey

The shading of the bars represents a simple index of association. For each type of group, the index scores a 0 for non-membership, a 1 for an inactive membership (like someone on the church rolls who no longer attends), and a 2 for active membership (someone who has been to a meeting recently); scores are then summed across the nine membership types. A score of 0 (white) on the index, then, means no memberships at all, a 1 (gray) means a single inactive membership, and a 2+ (black) means that the individual has at least two inactive memberships or at least one active membership—and possibly a lot more.

Note that the USA has the largest black area indicating a 2+ score (86% of respondents), and very nearly the lowest 0 score (7.8% compared to 6.4% for Sweden). This relatively strong performance against comparable societies in terms of amounts of voluntary association squares with the current professional literature on this topic1, but it also highlights the shortcomings of just looking at overall levels. Clearly, the differences between American society and, say, Japan are grounded in the sources of social capital that make up those societies. Their sources in American society elicit the General Patterns to which the heading refers.

The list of groups that will form our present measure of Voluntary Association is, in fact, twice as extensive as the World Values Survey measure. Taken from the Social Capital Community Benchmark Survey (SCCBS), it encompasses some eighteen types of groups:

"Do you participate in...
  1) an organization affiliated with religion?"
  2) a sports club, league, or outdoor activity?"
  3) a youth organization?"
  4) a parent association or other school support group?"
  5) a veterans group?"
  6) a neighborhood association?"
  7) a seniors group?"
  8) a charity or social welfare organization?"
  9) a labor union?"
  10) a professional, trade, farm or business association?"
  11) a service or fraternal organization?"
  12) an ethnic, nationality, or civil rights organization?"
  13) a political group?"
  14) a literary, art or musical group?"
  15) a hobby, investment or garden club?"
  16) a self-help program?"
  17) a group that meets over the internet?"
  18) other kinds of clubs or groups?"

These items were simply scored yes (0) vs. no (1), then summed to yield total Voluntary Association memberships. Figure 6.3 displays the overall membership profile for Americans in 2000. Note that 20.3% belong to no groups at all, but that more respondents are members of five or more groups (25.2%). The average adult American belongs to just about two and a half Voluntary Associations (2.537).

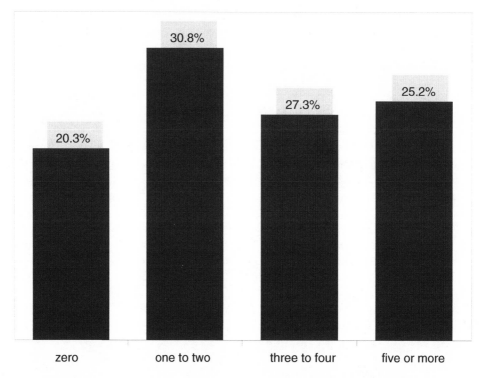

Figure 6.3 Voluntary Association membership profile of Americans in 2000

Sex

Is there sex role inequality in the social capital stock of Voluntary Association? In the aggregate, the answer is no. The rows in Table 6.1 are so closely matched that the sex difference for every membership column is under 4%.[2] Of course, there are sex differences in the *types* of memberships added up to form Voluntary Association, but they are mostly small and uninteresting (e.g., females are around 5% more likely to join literary/art/musical groups, whereas males are about 10% more likely to be members of a sports club).

Table 6.1 Sex and Voluntary Association

	No. of Group Memberships			
	0	1-2	3-4	5+
Male.	18.4%	30.7%	24.2%	26.6%
Female	22.0%	30.8%	23.3%	23.9%

n = 28,896

Much more interesting—and potentially important—is an activity from the same root word as *voluntary*, but without the *association*. "Volunteering" is defined in the SCCBS interview schedule as "…any unpaid work you've done to help people besides your family and friends or people you work with." Other studies have distinguished "informal helping" from "formal volunteering,"[3] and "individualistic-grounded volunteerism" from "collectivistic volunteerism"[4]; a recent review of the literature called volunteering "...an extension of private behavior into the public sphere."[5] It is defined in this fashion to unearth social capital not bound up in the box of formal group membership.

Figure 6.4 shows that enormous amounts of volunteering are offered in contemporary America. Well over half of all respondents (54.3%) pitched in over "the past twelve months"; 28.9% volunteered 1-9 times, and 25.4% volunteered at least 10 times (the number was capped at 53 for those who had volunteered more than weekly during the previous year). These total figures correspond closely to the results of other recent research,[6] but the present purpose concerns sex as a source of social capital more than it concerns aggregate amounts.

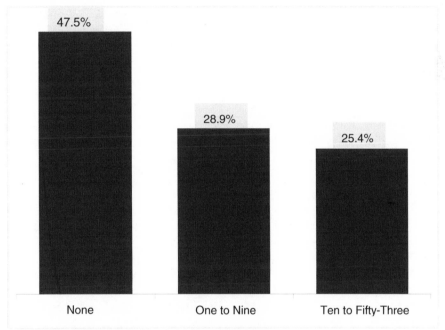

Figure 6.4 Volunteering profile of Americans in 2000
(Number of times volunteered over the past 12 months)

Turn, then, to Table 6.2 offering a gender comparison on volunteering. There is a real difference here.[7] Although the male predominance in the "none" column falls just below the 5% standard (it is 4.7%), a clear sex gap is apparent at the high end of volunteering (28.5% for females vs. 22.0% for males, a net of 5.5%). This margin of difference may not seem like much when viewed as a percentage, but it translates into millions more hours volunteered by American women.

Table 6.2 Sex and Volunteering

	No. of Times Volunteered (past year)		
	None	1-9	10-53
Male	48.2%	29.8%	22.0%
Female	43.5%	28.0%	28.5%

n = 28,984

Age

The power exerted by life stage over the forms of social capital has been well-established in previous chapters. Voluntary Association is not an exception to this sociological rule. Table 6.3 presents the familiar breakdown of age categories (< 30, 30-49, 50+) and the (now) familiar breakdown of group memberships (0, 1-2, 3-4, 5+). Notice this simple pattern: the middle-age and older rows match pretty well (i.e., within 2%), and both also well exceed the young adults row. Observe the 25.4% for the zero groups column for the youngsters while both upper cohorts are under 20% (17.7% and 19.7%, respectively). At the high end of Voluntary Association (5+), both sets of oldsters have at least 8% better participation rates than those under 30.[8] According to these SCCBS data, Americans generally step-up their Voluntary Association in the middle years of adulthood, and then sustain that level of commitment in their later years.

Table 6.3 Age and Voluntary Association

	No. of Group Memberships			
	0	1-2	3-4	5
< 30	25.4%	34.4%	21.9%	18.2%
30-49	17.7%	30.6%	25.0%	26.8%
50 +	19.7%	28.8%	23.7%	27.8%

$n = 28,167$

The first step in this life stage/Voluntary Association process is a well-known, widely evidenced phenomenon. Other studies, however, suggest a tail-off in group memberships in the later years of life, thus describing a curvilinear relationship between age and Voluntary Association. Summarizing his findings from three different datasets in *Bowling Alone*, Putnam puts it this way: "Civic engagement in general typically…[rises] from early adulthood toward a plateau in middle age, from which it gradually declines. This humpback pattern represents the natural arc of life's engagements."[9]

The fact that the SCCBS data do not reflect this "natural arc" bears two comments. First, it seems likely that the pattern depends on the checklist of groups offered to respondents. For example, one of the eighteen types making up our measure of Voluntary Association is "a seniors group," which does receive quite a surge in membership after age 50. Other datasets—like the GSS—that do not identify such groups might be reading a lateral move from soccer Mom to senior bowler as a decline by not picking up the latter membership. The second comment concerns Putnam's separation of age and cohort effects. At any given historical time point, the elderly bear the mark not only of their years, but also of the cultural patterns that differentiate them from younger generations. The very heart of Putnam's argument, in fact, is that current seniors constitute the "long civic generation" whose yeomanlike build-up of social capital is being depleted by the cohorts behind it. He specifically addresses this argument to the conundrum of volunteering:

Trends in volunteering over the last several decades are more complicated and in some respects more intriguing than the uniform decline that characterizes most dimensions of social capital in America in this period... By contrast, these same people [the "long civic generation"] report a steady *increase* in volunteering over this same period.[10]

In short, Putnam extends his argument by attempting to demonstrate (using DDB Needham Life Style data) that the lion's share of the increase in volunteering has issued forth from the "long civic generation" now in their later years.[11] While tabling a fuller discussion of life-stage/cohort effects for later, we arrive directly at the issue of age and volunteering.

Table 6.4 Age and Volunteering

	No. of Times Volunteered (past year)		
	None	1-9	10-53
< 30	45.8%	31.1%	23.1%
30-49	41.2%	31.5%	27.3%
50+	50.0%	25.0%	25.0%

n = 28,288

Note the oscillation in the zero column; non-volunteering drops nearly 5% in middle age, then rises significantly in older age. Although the age differences at the upper end of volunteering are unremarkable (23.1% to 27.3%), the overall effect fits the curvilinear, "natural arc of life's engagements" proposed by Putnam. This finding is further solidified by an extensive literature review that concludes: "Volunteering rises to its peak in middle age..."[12]

Education

In the introductory chapter to *Bowling Alone*, Putnam says that "Dozens of studies confirmed that education was by far the best predictor of engagement in civic life."[13] Moreover, the literature review referred to immediately above cites research showing that "Level of education is the most consistent predictor of volunteering."[14] The present prediction, therefore, is that education as a form of "human capital" will translate not only into occupational assets, but into this form of social capital as well.

So it does. Table 6.5 displays an education effect an order of magnitude beyond anything seen thus far. The 0 groups membership zone shrinks by over 30% (43.6% to 12.4%) and the 5 or more groups zone more than triples (9.2% to 32.6%) between the less than high school and college rows.[15] Turning immediately to Table 6.6, the dramatic effect for Voluntary Association is corroborated for Volunteering. Note that the zero-response is cut about in half (72.9% to 36.1%), and the 10-53 times zone nearly triples in size (11.5% to 30.7%) across the educational extremes.[16] Clearly, education is a prime mover in the appreciation of America's stock of social capital.

Table 6.5 Education and Voluntary Association

	No. of Group Memberships			
	0	1-2	3-4	5+
Less than high school	43.6%	33.5%	13.7%	9.2%
High school	27.5%	35.0%	21.5%	16.1%
College	12.4%	28.3%	26.7%	32.6%

n = 28,553

Table 6.6 Education and Volunteering

	No. of Times Volunteered (past year)		
	None	1-9	10-53
Less than high school	72.9%	15.6%	11.5%
High school	54.5%	25.6%	19.9%
College	36.1%	33.1%	30.7%

n = 28,676

Race

Given the immediately preceding set of findings and well-known education differences by race, one would be led to expect large black-white differences in voluntary association. In Table 6.7, not so much. In fact, black Americans appear to exceed white Americans in the "5+" category (29.9% to 25.4%), a not-quite-significant difference of 4.5%.

Table 6.7 Race and Voluntary Association

	No. of Group Memberships			
	0	1-2	3-4	5+
White	17.7%	31.4%	25.4%	25.4%
Black	20.6%	28.4%	21.1%	29.9%

n = 23,868

Table 6.8 does produce a racial contrast in the expected direction. White respondents exceed black respondents at the high end of informal helping by 8.3% (28.2% to 19.9%).

Table 6.8 Race and Volunteering

	No. of Times Volunteered (past year)		
	None	1-9	10-53
White	42.7%	29.1%	28.2%
Black	49.7%	30.3%	19.9%

n = 23,957

Race has shown itself to be a source of real variation in America's social capital.[17]

SOCIETAL TRENDS

But *is* that social capital stock appreciating? In particular, is it appreciating over the long-term periods recommended by financial—and sociological—analysts? And, most particularly, is it appreciating in the portfolio of voluntary association prized by pundits from Tocqueville to Putnam?

This is precisely the sort of question under critique in Chapter 1. The criticism, in short, is that the question needs to be *posed* more precisely. Averaging aggregate trends across a myriad of items can mask wild fluctuations in performance, whether the items are group memberships or Standard & Poor's stocks. So instead of applying multiple statistical controls to squeeze out some aggregate trend line, the present section surveys shifts *inside* known sources of social capital fluctuation.

Recall that the data for this longitudinal analysis are drawn from the cumulative General Social Survey. This data file permits the tracing of trends back to 1974.[18] The analysis here will present the familiar decade-by-decade breakdown (to downplay year-to-year fluctuations) crosstabulated by a new measure, Voluntary Association II. The latter has been built by adding up respondents' memberships in any-and-all of the following:

1) a fraternal group
2) a service group
3) a veterans group
4) a political club
5) a labor union
6) a sports club
7) a youth group
8) a school service group
9) a hobby club
10) a school fraternity
11) a nationality group
12) a farm organization
13) a literary or art group
14) a professional society
15) a church group
16) any other group

The summation yields lower total numbers than did the Voluntary Association measure built from the SCCBS data, so the breakdown here simply divides respondents with no (0), one (1) or two or more (2+) memberships.[19]

Sex

Tables 6.9a and b exhibit group memberships for American males and females over the past three decades. Note that in the 1970s just over half of American males (50.6%) had at least two group memberships, and that in the 1990s the comparable figure had "slipped" to just under half (49.7%). At the no-voluntary association end (0), there is some slippage (from 23.0% to 27.6%), but not enough to constitute a significant drop (only 4.6%). In the female subtable, no column varies by as much as 5%, although 2+ actually rises a (nonsignificant) 3.1%.[20] So: it looks like Voluntary Association II achieved a stationary state across recent decades for Americans of both sexes.

Table 6.9 Voluntary Association II by Decade for males and females

6.9a: Males

	No. of Group Memberships		
	0	1	2+
1970s	23.0%	26.4%	50.6%
1980s	26.1%	26.0%	48.0%
1990s	27.6%	22.8%	49.7%

n = 7,943

6.9b: Females

	No. of Group Memberships		
	0	1	2+
1970s	31.7%	28.1%	40.2%
1980s	34.6%	24.3%	41.1%
1990s	32.0%	24.6%	43.3%

n = 10,396

It is perfectly plausible, though, that non-joiner males and females are volunteering more, as suggested above. Unfortunately, no longitudinal record of informal helping is available in the GSS over the relevant period. To add further dimension to the findings from Table 6.9, the analysis will instead pursue a distinction suggested by both Chapter 4 and *Bowling Alone*.

Tables 6.10a and b show memberships in a subset of the groups that make up Voluntary Association II. Specifically, these tables sift for trends in Youth Group participation by adult GSS respondents. The latter measure simply sums memberships in "a youth group," "a school service group" and "a church group," then presents the totals in the same breakdown format (0, 1 or 2+) as in Tables 6.9a and b. This separate packaging of group types is strongly recommended by Chapter 4's findings about the decline of traditional family structures. Putnam explicitly draws the link between family status and these three group types:

> …two types of organizational affiliations, however, are sufficiently strongly related to marital and parental status to make a real difference in the aggregate: *church-* and *youth*-related activities… Not surprisingly, parents are also more involved in *school…* groups… [emphasis added].[21]

The creation of the Youth Groups measure (and the remaindered Non-Youth Groups measure below) permits a more nuanced scrutiny of Societal Trends.

Table 6.10 Youth Group Membership by Decade for males and females
6.10a: Males

	No. of Group Memberships		
	0	1	2+
1970s	59.9%	28.4%	11.7%
1980s	65.5%	25.7%	8.8%
1990s	63.6%	25.8%	10.6%

n = 8,277

6.10b: Females

	No. of Group Memberships		
	0	1	2+
1970s	49.3%	34.9%	15.8%
1980s	53.4%	32.6%	14.0%
1990s	54.5%	30.8%	14.7%

n = 10,798

Turning to Table 6.10a, there appears to be precious little appreciation or depreciation of Youth Group capital among American males. The 0 column does display a rise of over 5% between the 1970s and 1980s (59.9% to 65.5%), but then it dissipates to only a 3.7% net difference by the 1990s (59.9% to 63.6%). The same column, however, does reveal a trend in Table 10b.[22] American females are over 5% more likely to be members of no Youth Groups at all across the decades (49.3% up to 54.5%). Proper interpretation requires an immediate inspection of Table 6.11b, which certainly shows no evidence of decline in Non-Youth Groups. In fact, 0 membership slips while 2+ membership rises for females, which would constitute a nice, linear trend if the differences reached the 5% standard (they are 4.4% and 4.2%, respectively). The American male subtable 6.11a shows no detectable trend differences at all.[23]

Table 6.11 Non-Youth Group membership by Decade for males and females
6.11a: Males

	No. of Group Memberships		
	0	1	2+
1970s	31.0%	30.0%	39.0%
1980s	32.2%	28.4%	39.3%
1990s	34.2%	26.9%	39.0%

n = 7,962

6.11b: Females

| | No. of Group Memberships | | |
	0	1	2+
1970s	51.7%	24.9%	23.4%
1980s	51.2%	23.7%	25.1%
1990s	47.3%	25.1%	27.6%

n = 10,417

The breakdown into Youth and Non-Youth types of voluntary association produced the only significant change in this series of tables: American women are just about 5% less likely to have been members of youth groups in the Nineties than in the Seventies, which seems relatively modest given the drops in family commitment charted in Chapter 4. Furthermore, it seems as though females are compensating by joining (somewhat) more Non-Youth groups. Male patterns of voluntary association later appear pretty much as they did sooner.

Age

A quick read of Societal Trends by age tells a pretty simple tale. The Voluntary Association II tables for young adults and older adults have no story—that is, no significant shifts in percentages at all. Table 6.12b, though, speaks volumes in the 0 column. There is a 6.3% increase in 30-49 year old Americans belonging to no group at all, the largest single shift seen thus far.[24]

Table 6.12
Voluntary Association II by Decade for young, middle-aged and older adults
6.12a: Less than 30

| | No. of Group Memberships | | |
	0	1	2+
1970s	35.2%	26.4%	38.4%
1980s	37.6%	23.2%	39.3%
1990s	36.1%	23.5%	40.4%

n = 4,380

6.12b: 30-49

| | No. of Group Memberships | | |
	0	1	2+
1970s	22.8%	25.1%	52.2%
1980s	28.3%	22.9%	48.8%
1990s	29.1%	20.8%	50.1%

n = 7,088

6.12c: 50+

	No. of Group Memberships		
	0	1	2+
1970s	27.4%	30.2%	42.4%
1980s	29.4%	28.3%	42.3%
1990s	28.3%	27.9%	43.8%

n = 6,806

Table 6.13 Youth Group membership by Decade for young, middle-aged and older adults
6.13a: Less than 30

	No. of Group Memberships		
	0	1	2+
1970s	66.0%	23.8%	10.3%
1980s	66.6%	22.9%	10.4%
1990s	64.8%	23.0%	12.3%

n = 4,515

6.13b: 30-49

	No. of Group Memberships		
	0	1	2+
1970s	47.3%	29.3%	23.5%
1980s	56.7%	25.7%	17.6%
1990s	57.2%	24.5%	18.3%

n = 7,382

6.13c: 50+

	No. of Group Memberships		
	0	1	2+
1970s	52.1%	40.0%	7.8%
1980s	55.4%	38.1%	6.5%
1990s	56.4%	36.7%	6.9%

n = 7,114

Since the Voluntary Association II measure in these tables is the simple combination of Youth Groups and Non-Youth Groups, those components may now be examined separately for further clues. There turns out to be no mystery. Table 6.13b is clearly the culprit. The non-membership column of Youth Groups swells a suspicious 9.9% (47.3% to 57.2%); the suspicions are confirmed as the highest membership category drops 5.2% (from 23.5% to 18.3% in the 2+ column). Remarkable innocence is testified to by all other tables in this array. No other 1970s-1990's difference amounts to as much as 5%.[25]

Table 6.14 Non-Youth Group membership by Decade for young, middle-aged and older adults
6.14a: Less than 30

	No. of Group Memberships		
	0	1	2+
1970s	46.3%	26.0%	27.7%
1980s	46.1%	25.0%	28.9%
1990s	46.0%	25.8%	28.2%

n = 4,389

6.14b: 30-49

	No. of Group Memberships		
	0	1	2+
1970s	38.0%	28.2%	38.8%
1980s	40.0%	26.3%	33.7%
1990s	39.1%	26.3%	34.6%

n = 7,098

6.14c: 50+

	No. of Group Memberships		
	0	1	2+
1970s	43.8%	27.2%	29.0%
1980s	44.3%	25.6%	30.1%
1990s	42.7%	25.4%	31.8%

n = 6,827

Summing up the story: the real villain of the piece is an abandonment of Youth Groups by 30-49 year old Americans over the past three decades.

Education

Our General Patterns sections have shown that sex and age are shapers of social capital, but that education is a mighty forge. Is education also a crucible of Societal Trends?

In the broadest comparison of Voluntary Association II, Table 6.15a posts a clear drop in memberships among Americans at the lowest educational level. It is manifest in the 6.3% increase of respondents with less than a high school degree who belong to no groups at all (from 39.3% to 45.6% in the 0 column). Table 6.15b shows a parallel change of 8.6% in the 0 column for high school graduates (24.8% to 33.4%), as well as a drop in the 2+ column of 6.8% (48.2% down to 41.4%). Among college respondents, by contrast, no numbers shift more than 3%, thus showing no apparent change in Table 6.15c.[26]

Table 6.15 Voluntary Association II by Decade for levels of education
6.15a: Less than high school

	No. of Group Memberships		
	0	1	2+
1970s	39.3%	32.3%	28.4%
1980s	47.0%	28.9 %	24.1%
1990s	45.6%	28.4%	26.0%

n = 5,089

6.15b: High school

	No. of Group Memberships		
	0	1	2+
1970s	24.8%	27.0%	48.2%
1980s	29.7%	26.0%	44.3%
1990s	33.4%	25.2%	41.4%

n = 9,419

6.15c: College

	No. of Group Memberships		
	0	1	2+
1970s	12.0%	17.6%	70.4%
1980s	14.4%	17.8%	67.9%
1990s	13.4%	18.0%	68.5%

n = 3,803

The Table 6.16 series specifies the trend analysis for Youth Groups, and the first two subtables hold to form. Again non-participators swell significantly in the left-hand columns of 6.17a and 6.17b, but now there is a borderline effect in the college subtable. The drop in the 2+ column of subtable 6.16c is 5.8% across the 1970s (25.0%) and 1980s (19.2%), but as of the 1990s the gap is only 4.7% (25.0% to 20.3%).[27]

Table 6.16 Youth Group membership by Decade for levels of education
6.16a: Less than high school

	No. of Group Memberships		
	0	1	2+
1970s	61.7%	31.6%	6.7%
1980s	67.9%	27.6 %	4.5%
1990s	69.7%	25.2%	5.2%

n = 5,259

6.16b: High school

	No. of Group Memberships		
	0	1	2+
1970s	51.6%	32.9%	15.5%
1980s	57.5%	30.1%	12.4%
1990s	60.9%	27.0%	12.1%

n = 9,787

6.16c: College

	No. of Group Memberships		
	0	1	2+
1970s	45.0%	30.0%	25.0%
1980s	50.1%	30.8%	19.2%
1990s	45.4%	34.3%	20.3%

n = 3,999

Non-Youth Group memberships are somewhat less volatile. There are no changes near the 5% standard in Table 6.17a, but another detectable surge of 6.2% in non-membership among high school grads (39.7% to 45.9%). The college subtable shows a drop-off at the high end of membership that just makes the cut at 5.4% (in the "2+" column, 58.1% to 52.7%).[28]

Table 6.17 Non-Youth Group membership by Decade for levels of education
6.17a: Less than high school

	No. of Group Memberships		
	0	1	2+
1970s	58.1%	25.4%	16.4%
1980s	62.8%	22.9%	14.2%
1990s	60.5%	24.0%	15.6%

n = 5,098

6.17b: High school

	No. of Group Memberships		
	0	1	2+
1970s	39.7%	29.0%	31.3%
1980s	42.6%	27.9%	29.6%
1990s	45.9%	26.3%	27.8%

n = 9,442

6.17c: College

	No. of Group Memberships		
	0	1	2+
1970s	16.8%	25.1%	58.1%
1980s	20.0%	24.0%	56.0%
1990s	21.0%	26.3%	52.7%

n = 3,811

Several generalizations are warranted. First, evidence of a decline in voluntary association is much stronger at lower levels of education. Five of the six subtables for both the high school non-graduates and high school graduates show real declines, some approaching double figure percentages. The trend for college respondents is not there in the overall for Voluntary Association II, and barely borders on 5% in the Youth and Non-Youth subtables. Second, the General Patterns of education swamp its Societal Trends. Observe how heavily the subtables shift to the right through each series above. The movement across the columns at each higher education level is so pronounced that the college subtable of Voluntary Association II (6.15c) has over two-thirds of its cases in the highest membership level (2+) compared to only about one in four for less than high school respondents. Clearly, education is a much more potent generator of social capital than it is a focuser of trends. The third generalization concerns the limits of the present form of analysis. Although it is useful (I would argue indispensable) to assay social capital at the basic variable-by-variable level, it is a mistake to stop there. Determining whether the rate for turning human capital into social capital has changed can obscure more global changes in human capital itself. Table 6.18 displays just such a global change in educational level in America across the past three decades.

Table 6.18

	Level of Education		
	Less than high school	High school	College
1970s	35.7%	49.2%	15.2%
1980s	26.5%	51.9%	21.5%
1990s	17.2%	53.5%	29.4%

n = 37,981

The share of college respondents very nearly doubled (15.2% to 29.4%), while high school non-graduate respondents were more than cut in half (35.7% to 17.2%). Further analyses (not shown) reveal that the educational upgrade has been concentrated in the 30-49 age group—the very segment of the American population with the biggest *drop* in voluntary association since the 1970s. What is sorely needed to take account of these complex trends and countertrends is a simplifying device—a Model of Social Capital.

7

The Model of Social Capital

The internet is overrun with treasure-seekers. There are websites galore devoted to geographic analyses, excavation tips, and even new technologies. A recent article entitled "Satellites Hunt for Buried Treasure"[1] describes a microwave radar system developed by NASA that can detect underground objects from outer space. Let us suppose that this magical breakthrough inspires a project to chart all the underground valuables on Earth—a comprehensive Treasure Map, if you will.

There are complications. First of all, what counts as "treasure"? Gold bullion certainly qualifies, but how about ceramic vases from ancient civilizations? The myriad of buried objects would require some classification scheme to lay out the basic types of treasure and distinguish them on the map. Complication number two concerns how these types would relate to one another. Discovering El Dorado might devalue Spanish coins by flooding the world gold market, while hyping the value of the local Aztec statues. Third, since mapping the planet is a titanic task (even excluding wrecks like the Titanic), it would be necessary to have some model of the factors that generate treasure such as burial sites or precious metal mines. What one needs, in short, is a *theory of buried treasure*.

The present assay concerns social capital. Each of the four major types of this treasure have been counted, weighed and catalogued, but each presents a partial picture. Again and again the analyses have encountered limits bordering the other forms of social capital. American women are more likely to be unmarried with children than American men, but does this factor into their friendships? Americans of both sexes are working more than before, which has implications—as yet unevidenced—for voluntary group membership. Without overtaxing our analogy, the *pattern* of buried treasure must be unearthed to evaluate the trove before one can make any sense of the whole. This chapter is devoted to charting that pattern.

PUTTING THE MODEL TOGETHER

Figure 7.1 has been lifted directly from Chapter 1. Essentially, it is a picture of my assertion that these four "zones" of social capital need to be conceptualized together. Now it is time to produce the data that will materialize the connecting arrows.

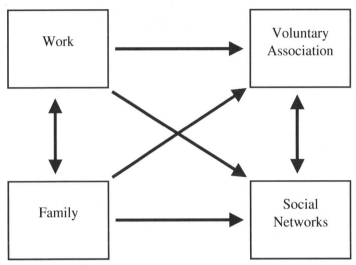

Figure 7.1

Family Structure and Work

Note that the vertical arrow at left is double-pointed. This is a simple signal that effects may flow both ways—i.e., family responsibilities may affect hours worked *and* hours worked may affect investments in family life. Both are true; both are unsurprising. A lavish literature from scholarly articles to supermarket magazines describes the complex relations between work and family to the point that basic documentation is not required here. But since model-building is the task at hand, this well-charted arrow will serve to introduce the analytical approach.

The approach will lean heavily on the direct display of effect lines. Since the argument throughout has been for showing social capital rather than hiding it behind statistical formulas, and since the last four chapters have shown the power of sex, age and education over the levels of social capital, the technique to be applied here is multiple analyses of variance.[2] It is sophisticated enough to incorporate several variables into the model at a time, while also being readily understood in graphical displays such as Figure 7.2.

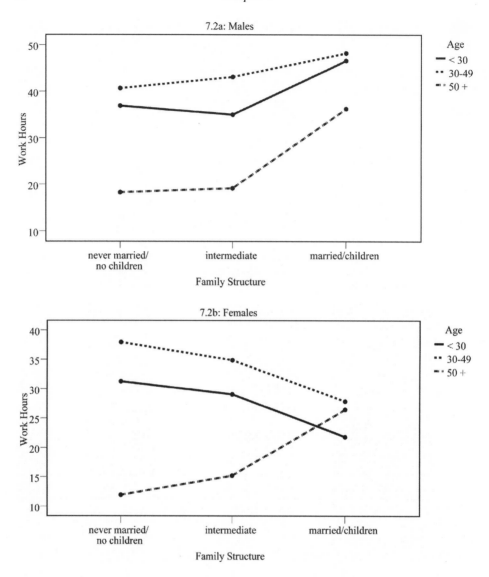

Figure 7.2 Work Hours by Family Structure for males and females

Before talking numbers, simply observe the tilt of the lines which are anchored by dots representing average hours worked. In 7.2a for males, the lines pretty much rise to the right. There is a slight dropoff in the middle for young males, but at every age the married with children status towers above the rest. In fact, men fifty and over in the latter status nearly double the work hours of those who are unmarried with no children.[3] The midpoint of Family Structure is listed as intermediate. This somewhat vague term is needed to collapse several different family statuses together. Specifically, respondents who are once married with children, once married without children, never married with children and married without children (in the home) are now considered together. All of these family statuses have been separately analyzed in Chapter 4, and here are viewed as intermediate between the non-investment in family life at left and the full investment in family life at right.

Now notice the differing heights of the lines. This is a reflection of the "age-graded" nature of work discussed in Chapter 3. The bottom line in both grids is for 50+ Americans, and hard-working, mid-career 30-49 year olds are at top as expected. But the real news here is a sex-specific effect. By vivid contrast with males of the same life-stage, women in the younger age groups average less work with more family investment, and the drop-off is especially pronounced in the married with children status. Not so for older females. Those with full family responsibilities in the 50+ category more than double the work effort of the women at left.[4]

Figure 7.2 nicely demonstrates the rationale for using MANOVA in this analysis. Here we see a male-female difference in how Family Structure relates to work, but it is not a simple difference. The generally positive effects of family on work for men and negative effects for women switch radically for the latter after age 50. So the effect is doubly dependent: it depends on sex *and* age, which is what statisticians call an interaction effect.[5] Happily, the demonstration is visually apparent as well as statistically significant.

The multiple analysis of variance that produced Figure 7.2 entered Family Structure as the "independent variable" and work hours as the "dependent variable." In everyday language, family responsibilities are viewed as driving work. A reverse effect is also more than plausible. As is implied by the downward point of the arrow in Figure 7.1, work commitments may also drive family commitments.

This alternate view of the (same) data is shown in Figure 7.3. Here the dots represent an average based on a score of 0 for never married without children, 1 for intermediates, and 2 for married with children; a higher average, therefore, means respondents committing themselves more to family life, whereas a lower average (i.e., a lower dot) means lesser family commitments. Figure 7.3a displays an upper incline to the right for all male lines. That is, harder working males have higher levels of family commitment. In 7.3b, on the other hand, there is a pronounced drop in the female line depicting ages 30-49. This suggests a negative association of work and family during the prime child-rearing years for women.[6]

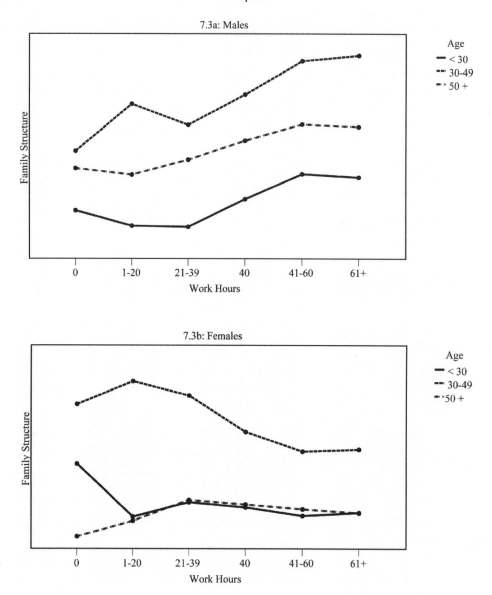

Figure 7.3 Family Structure by Work Hours for males and females

Voluntary Association and Social Networks

The vertical arrow at the right of Figure 7.1 is also double-pointed. Though considerable sociological scholarship[7] has been devoted to the interchange of voluntary association and social networks, this is less on the public mind than is the family-work issue. In part, this is because groups and relationships are considered private business rather than public institutions. As Chapter 2 argued, though, both of these zones are indispensable assets in society's capital stock and indispensable assets for personal well-being. So how do they connect?

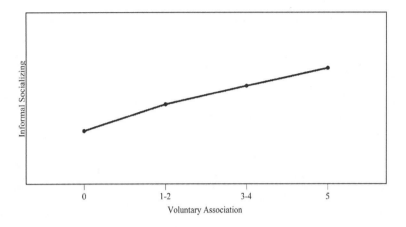

Figure 7.4 Informal Socializing by Voluntary Association

Powerfully and positively. Figure 7.4 shows a single line steadily rising to the right. Since the horizontal axis quantifies group memberships using the Voluntary Association measure (from Chapter 6), and since the vertical axis is an overall measure of Informal Socializing,[8] the interpretation is straightforward: people with more group memberships also tend to hang out more with their social networks. This is true at every age, for both sexes, and even when statistical adjustments are made for education, which itself powerfully affects both groups and relationships.[9] Figure 7.5 again reverses the effect to test the double-sidedness of the arrow, and again the test is passed. As Informal Socializing rises, so does the average level of Voluntary Association in an effect which is clearly confirmed both statistically and visually.[10]   In concrete terms, "high"

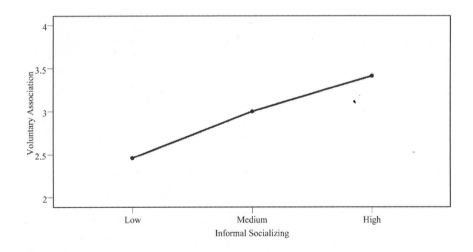

Figure 7.5 Voluntary Association by Informal Socializing

socializing Americans average a full group membership more than "low" socializers.[11] It would appear that social networks and voluntary associations are social capital assets that tend to appreciate together.

Work and Voluntary Association

When people say they are "too busy" to join an exercise club or go to the movies, they generally mean that work and family commitments have tied them down. By implication, those responsibilities must be taken care of before other forms of social capital may be pursued. The boxes on the left of Figure 7.1 are viewed as primary and required; those on the right are seen as secondary and elective. Everybody knows that attending meetings and helping friends are important, but one must "take care of business" first.

This primary/secondary distinction in the forms of social capital is also reflected in the direction of the arrows in the middle of Figure 7.1. First consider the top horizontal arrow. In both the "too busy" idea and in the arguments against American workaholism, the assumption is that the hours on the job erode secondary forms of social capital. Is this assumption correct?

The answer is no. Figure 7.6 shows a relationship between Work Hours and Voluntary Association that is *not* uniformly negative. The bottom of the grid breaks down hours into groupings familiar from Chapter 3; the vertical axis measures the variation in average Voluntary Association that is, likewise, familiar. The line in the Figure itself has special qualities. It represents the relationship taking into account the sex, age and education level of respondents.[12] The multiple analysis of variance technique that both produces the effect line and tests its significance has an additional benefit. It allows us to keep an eye on whether the basic size and shape of the relationship changes for different types of Americans.

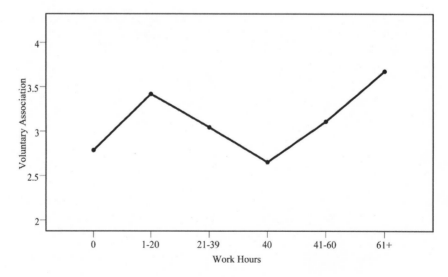

Figure 7.6 Voluntary Association by Work Hours

Now back to the effect line itself. In a resounding rejection of simple answers when it comes to questions about social capital, there really are three separate effects. There is a clear climb in Voluntary Association differentiating non-
working respondents from those working 1-20 hours per week. Then the dots
drop through 21-39 hours to a lower average among 40 hours respondents. The
average then rises again to reach its peak at the 61+ work hours extreme.

There is no question of the statistical or substantive reality of these effects. Giv-
en that the overall average for American adults is membership in 3 groups,[13] the
swing of a full group between 0 hours (mean = 2.707) and 61+ hours (mean = 3.701)
is remarkable. Also remarkable is the low point of membership at 40 hours (mean =
2.597). Traditional "full time" workers do even less Voluntary Association than non-
working respondents. And the respondents with the most credible claims of being
"too busy" at work do the most Voluntary Association of anyone.

The next step in the analysis will follow the lead of Chapter 6 by breaking down
overall memberships into Youth Group (youth + school + church) and Non-Youth
Group (all other) participation. Figure 7.7 presents youth groups first. The effect line
generally imitates Figure 7.6, but the variation is weaker.[14] To some degree this reflects a numerical limit. Since it is built from only 3 group types, the totals for the
Youth Group index are low; the overall average of .579 bespeaks the fact that many
Americans are members of none of these groups at all. Nevertheless, the double-
peak pattern does appear. No hours and 40 hours are low points, 1-20 and 61+ hours
are peaks. Separate analyses (not shown) indicate that this pattern is a bit stronger for
women and for 30-49 year olds, which would suggest—not surprisingly—that the
double peak might be related to family life.

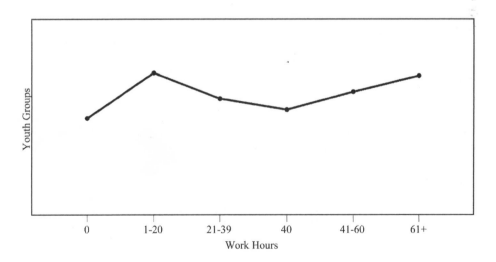

Figure 7.7 Youth Group membership by Work Hours

Figure 7.8 shows an even more pronounced oscillation than Figure 7.7. Statistical significance is not an issue, and substantive significance even less so.[15]
Consider: the average 1-20 hour worker has about half a membership more than

a typical 40 hour worker (2.568 versus 2.052, respectively); 61+ hour workers average nearly a full membership more than the latter (2.993 versus 2.052, respectively). And remember, these differences are based on only a subset of the overall Voluntary Association measure. The double-peak effect is somewhat greater for males (not shown). So: the response to work hours is greater for females with Youth Groups, and greater for males with Non-Youth Groups.

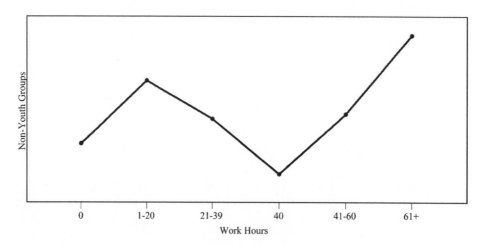

Figure 7.8 Non-Youth Group membership by Work Hours

Some larger conclusions are in order as well. The notion of work as uniformly corrosive of social capital has received no support. *All* effect lines rise with labor force entry. For reasons still unclear, part-time workers perform more voluntary association than do full-time workers. And "workaholics" putting in over 40 hours per week are the most actively associational of all.

Work and Social Networks

The term "workaholic" is borrowed from the field of addiction, which by definition involves an unhealthy neglect of parts of one's life. Perhaps work promotes that neglect in the most private zone of social capital—one's social network.

Figure 7.9 displays the work pattern for the number of close friends measure utilized in Chapter 5.[16] Frankly, there is not much of a pattern with the exception of the now familiar dip at 40 hours. The source of that familiarity, of course, is the immediately preceding set of findings concerning voluntary association. And since Figures 7.4 and 7.5 showed a close network-membership connection, there is a reassuring consistency within the evidence of the model. That reassurance, unfortunately, does not dissipate the growing mystery of low sociality among full time workers.

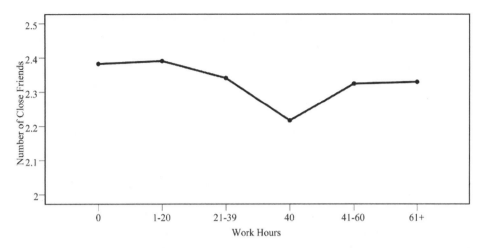

Figure 7.9 Number of Close Friends by Work Hours

The second area of detail in the social network concerns kin. In response to "How many times in the past 12 months have you visited relatives in person or had them visit you?" scores ranged from 0 to 53. In this case, though, it is instructive to separately display the sex effect lines in Figure 7.10. Three features of the figure are noteworthy. First, the female line is well above the male line across the entire range of work hours. American women visit kin an average of up to 5 times more per year than men at a given level of work. Second, both sexes do show signs of the drop off at full-time status, although for males it extends through 21-39 to 40 hours, whereas for females it just dips at 40. Third, the overall track of the trend lines is up to the right, such that 61+ hour workers visit kin about 4 times a year *more* than non-workers.[17] Again the data do not support the idea that work is caustic to other forms of social capital.

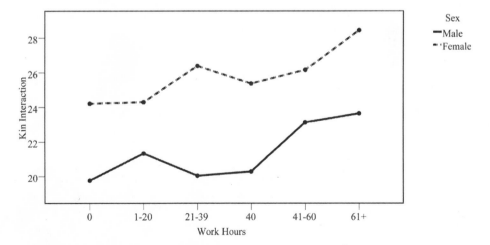

Figure 7.10 Kin Interaction by Work Hours

Work and neighboring have both been shown to be dynamic areas. In a nutshell from Chapters 3 and 5, work hours are clearly up and social evenings spent with neighbors are clearly down across America. Before the trend analysis of Chapter 8, then, it is important to chart the form of their relationship to each other. Figure 7.11 shows important differences in that form by age.[18] The item "How often do you talk with or visit your immediate neighbors?" offered responses from never (1) to just about everyday (7). All categories averaged from just over 4 to just over 5, which means most Americans neighbor from once to several times a month. Older Americans have the highest averages across the board, and work is associated with less neighboring for them. There are two contrasts with younger Americans. In the first place, note that respondents under 30 neighbor at rates well below respondents over 50. This is a switch from Chapter 5, but the reversal appears to be a function of the more informal "talk with or visit" wording here compared to the go-out-to-hang-out implication of the GSS "spend a social evening with a neighbor" item. The second point of contrast is in the work-neighboring trend, which here is clearly upward for twentysomethings. The 30-49 year old respondents in the middle show some evidence of the double-peak pattern with high points at 1-20 and 41-60 hours. The age-sensitivity of the work-neighboring relationship will bear watching in the analyses to follow.

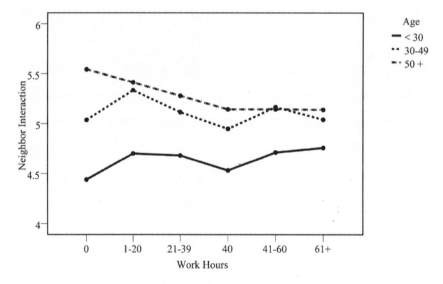

Figure 7.11 Neighbor Interaction by Work Hours

Also worth watching is the supplementary analysis shown in Figure 7.12. It is supplementary in the sense that it goes beyond our usual breakdown of social network areas. This projection of responses to the "How many times in the past 12 months have you socialized with coworkers outside of work?" item again is based on the multiple analysis of variance technique complete with controls for sex, age and education, but all of this statistical machinery is not even necessary.

Coworker socializing rises rapidly with work hours, topping out at nearly 17 occasions a year for 61+ hour workers.[19] "Workaholics" actually build up a whole new zone of the social network with their "addiction."

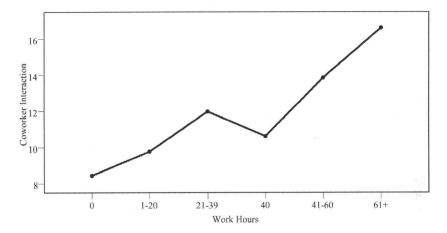

Figure 7.12 Co-worker Interaction by Work Hours

Family Structure and Social Networks

Everyday phrases like "swinging singles," "soccer moms" and "empty nesters" all touch on the same everyday reality: family life stages set the stage for the rest of one's social life. This is the rationale for the bottom arrow in Figure 7.1. To check its substance, we depart from a piecemeal approach to overview all three network areas together. The three panels of Figure 7.13 tell a coherent story: investment in family structure decreases friendship, really increases kin visiting, and bumps up neighboring.

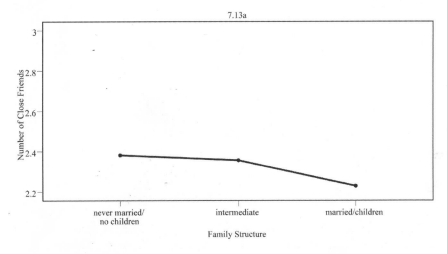

Figure 7.13 Social Network Interaction by Family Structure (*continued next page*)

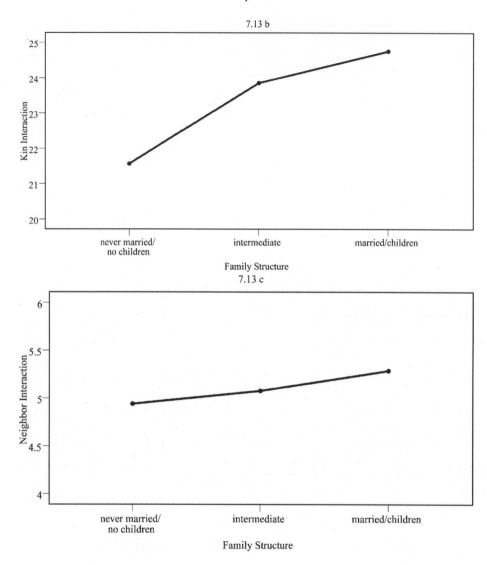

Figure 7.13 Social Network Interaction by Family Structure

Figure 7.13a shows a slight drop in hanging out with friends accompanying the mixed family investment here called intermediate, and then a bit more change with the fuller commitment of being married with children; this effect is statistically significant, but given the fact that Family Structure here measures children residing in the home, the difference of less than .2 in averages seems a modest drop for active parents.[20] Figure 7.13b displays the number of visits with relatives during the previous year. Here, each greater family commitment translates into a few more kin get-togethers.[21] In Figure 7.13c, neighboring increases pretty steadily with increases in family commitment.[22] Clearly, there is a real but varying connection between the bottom two zones of the Model of Social Capital.

Family Structure and Voluntary Association

The final arrow in the model connects two pet topics of people with a dim view of the state of America. Editorial writers, talking heads and daytime talk show hosts take it as a given that societal disintegration starts with a neglect of family and community life. In all likelihood, this is the operating assumption behind the widespread sense that America is going downhill, as revealed in the public opinion polls summarized in Chapter 1. Widespread though it may be, this is quite a complex proposition that demands data about how these pillars of society connect.

Throughout this model-building exercise, the analysis has punctuated its summaries of social capital connections with what are technically known as "interaction effects." That phrase has been avoided for fear of confusion with a subject matter that is, after all, about social interaction, but now it demands a spotlight. Essentially, a statistical interaction happens when an effect differs for different types of people. In Figure 7.11, for instance, the work-neighboring effect differed so much for different age groups that, a) it was necessary to show them separately because, b) there was a significant interaction effect.

That example was used because age is involved in an even more dramatic interaction effect here. Consider the conundrum of Figure 7.14. Proceeding with the familiar logic of the analysis, it would appear that the effects of Family Structure differ, well, dramatically by age. The interaction effect boils down to this: more family involvement does not meaningfully increase involvement in groups for the young (bottom line), increases it a little for the middle-aged (middle line), and increases it a lot for older respondents (top line). There is an alternate way to think about this same effect. First of all, most Americans do not get married and have children *after* age 50. Second, most people spend a considerable period of time in a given family status, up to most of a lifetime for those who remain married. Therefore, third, perhaps age should be viewed as *acting upon* a given family status rather than the reverse.

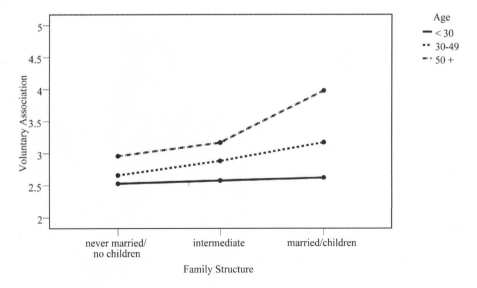

Figure 7.14 Voluntary Association by Family Structure

The switch in analytical perspectives brings us to Figure 7.15. All three sets of lines display versions of the same interaction effect. Starting with 7.15b, as married Americans with children hit middle age, their involvement with youth groups nearly doubles, then does not change over age 50. Americans with no family involvement slip a bit in ages 30-49, and also stay at that level when older. Intermediate family involvement is associated with a small rise in middle age, and a clear drop in the older age category. So: age acts upon Youth Group membership with little effect for never marrieds without children, a major effect for marrieds with children, and an intermediate effect for those of intermediate family status.[23] The details differ, but the interaction effect in 7.15c is the same in essence. All three lines charting Non-Youth Group membership climb through ages 30-49, but then their slopes steepen more for those with greater family commitments.[24] The combined effect in 7.15a is truly dramatic. Americans un-invested in family life show very gradual and very slight gains in groups with age; intermediate investors in family show a substantive gain in middle age, then little additional gain; major family investors *make gains in membership of nearly a full group at each upward step in age.*[25] It would appear that maturation means more community commitment the more family commitments one makes.

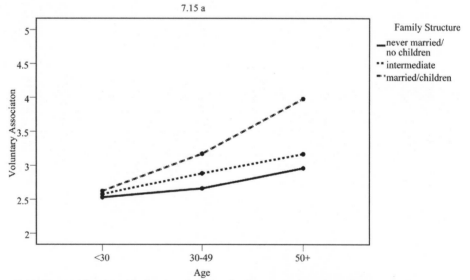

Figure 7.15 Group Membership by Age for Family Structure (*continued next page*)

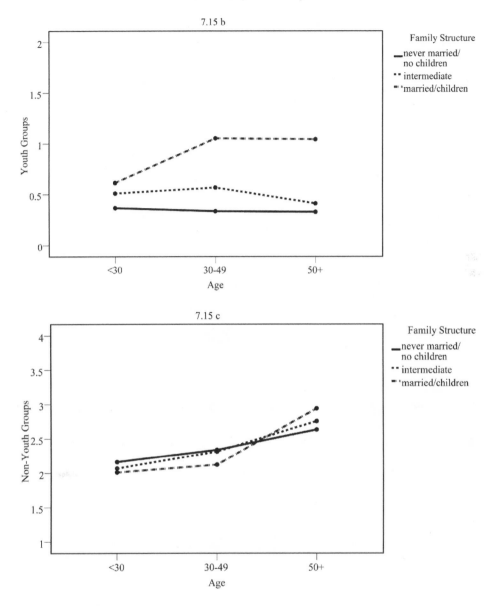

Figure 7.15 Group Membership by Age for Family Structure

After a chapter too packed with findings to simply summarize, it will be useful to return to the simple display of Figure 7.1. It is now a full-fledged Model of Social Capital in three senses. First, every arrow has been amply documented with data. Second, like any useful model, it has produced unanticipated findings such as the double-peak effect of work and the family-age interaction. Third and finally, the model spells out the dangers of disconnecting the forms of social capital when taking the more complex step of tracking their trends over time.

8

Modeling Trends

What good is a treasure map that is out of date? If the Treasure of Sierra Madre has already been unburied, that needs to be so indicated on the map. If the value of copper artifacts has been rising relative to gold, that is important information for prospectors. The buried treasure that is the social capital of American society has just been charted, but it needs to be tracked over time.

For this purpose, the analysis now turns to the cumulative General Social Survey to screen for trends. The word "screen" is used advisedly, however. The dense lines interconnecting the four forms of social capital in the model are not to be dissolved in order to produce some average trajectory. In fact, this trend analysis will commence by reproducing the model elements of Chapter 7 and adding a time component.

TRENDS IN THE MODEL OF SOCIAL CAPITAL

In essence, the Figures from Chapter 7 will be reproduced here with a visual (and statistical) representation of the effects by decade. To introduce the analysis with an overview of Societal Trend findings to date, consider the annotated Figure 8.1. The arrows in the boxes are simplified summaries of the findings in Chapters 3, 4, 5, and 6. Subject to the qualifications to be found in the many tables in those chapters, the basic trends in American society are as follows: work hours are up, family structure is down, voluntary association has fluctuated little, and social network interaction is basically stable for relatives, tending upwards for friends, but down quite a bit for neighbors. These simple trends in each box now need to be reconsidered in terms of the *linkages between* the components of social capital.

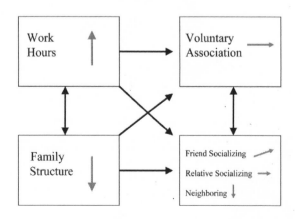

Figure 8.1

Family Structure and Work

In parallel with Chapter 7, Figure 8.2 probes the left-hand vertical arrow in the model. As will be the case throughout, there is a separate line displaying the effect for each decade. Observe that all three lines rise to the right in 8.2a and decline to the right in 8.2b. This is the familiar finding of more investment in family by males working more hours and less by females working more hours. Though the slope of the lines appear to be in rough parallel across the decades, this is a case where the statistical machinery can be applied to detect a subtle shift. Start with the obvious and unsubtle: the lines have been shifting downwards. Note the clear, progressive separation in Figure 8.2a. This means, in effect, lesser investment in family at each level

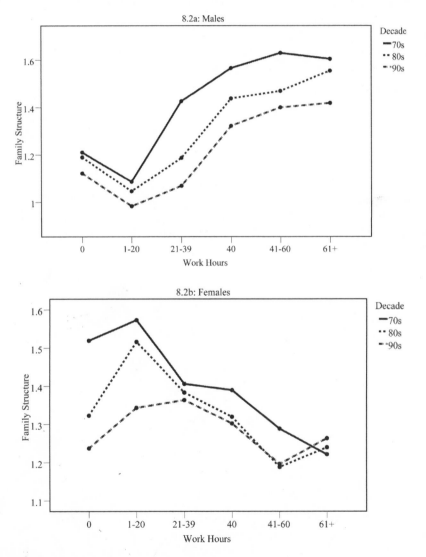

Figure 8.2 Family Structure by Work Hours over time

of work by American males. The downward shift is less apparent for American females and that—along with the significant interaction effect—is the tip-off.[1] Note that the 1990s line in 8.2b has *not* clearly separated from the 1980s, and, slopewise, it is simply flatter than the other two. It would appear that the negative association of work hours and family life is becoming progressively weaker for American women.

Voluntary Association and Social Networks

As the counterpart to the overall measure of Informal Socializing for Figure 4 in Chapter 7, an index of the same name has been built here by combining the "spend a social evening" GSS items for friends, relatives and neighbors. The present Figure 8.3 mirrors the central finding of a positive feedback loop connecting groups and networks. The steeply rising slant of the average-socializing-per-membership line here has the additional dimension of time. Again the slopes are about the same, but the later lines are a bit under the 1970s. Most of the drop is accounted for by less neighboring, a point to be elaborated below. There is no serious question in the statistical tests undergirding Figure 8.3 that Voluntary Association II is strongly associated with Informal Socializing, and those tests yield no evidence that the nature of that association has changed much since the 1970s.[2] The right-hand vertical arrow in the social capital model remains intact.

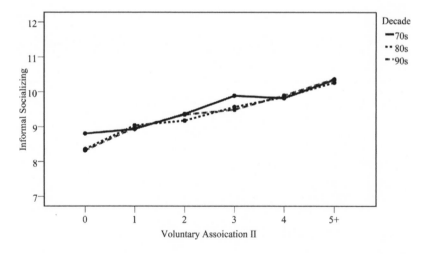

Figure 8.3 Informal Socializing by Voluntary Association II over time

Work and Voluntary Association

One of the major benefits of using both the Social Capital Community Benchmark Survey and the General Social Survey is confirmation: if the same effect appears in both studies, there is additional assurance that it really appears in American society. Another major benefit transcends mere replication. The longitudinal track of the GSS allows inspection of findings from the SCCBS to determine whether they are long-standing or recent phenomena.

Figure 8.4 puts the latter benefit in bold relief. The "double peak" pattern connecting work hours to voluntary association (see Chapter 7) is in evidence, *but it appears to be emergent over time*. All three lines rise with part-time work hours, dip in the middle, and then rise again at the upper end of work. Note, though, how the dot for average group memberships for 1-20 hours pops up a bit from the 1970s to the 1980s, then really rises in the 1990s. This is the change that creates a clear double peak effect.

Breaking down Voluntary Association II into Youth and Non-Youth groups turns up the magnification on the nature of this change. Figure 8.5 shows the double peak pattern, but there is no clear spike up over time for Youth group membership.[3] Figure 8.6, on the other hand, shows exactly that. Males working 1-20 hours per week rise slightly in the Eighties, then skyrocket in the Nineties; the net difference in averages in 8.6a is over half a group membership. The change for females is much more modest (about a fifth of a group), but still apparent. It looks like the first peak in Voluntary Association among part-time workers has been driven up by greatly increased membership among American males and somewhat increased membership among American females in Non-Youth groups.[4]

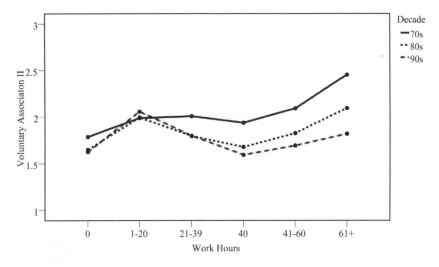

Figure 8.4 Voluntary Association II by Work Hours over time

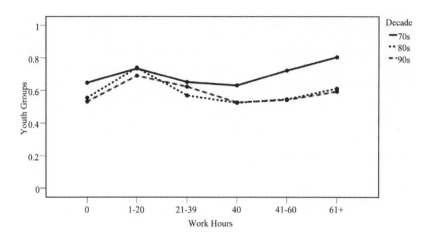

Figure 8.5 Youth Group membership by Work Hours over time

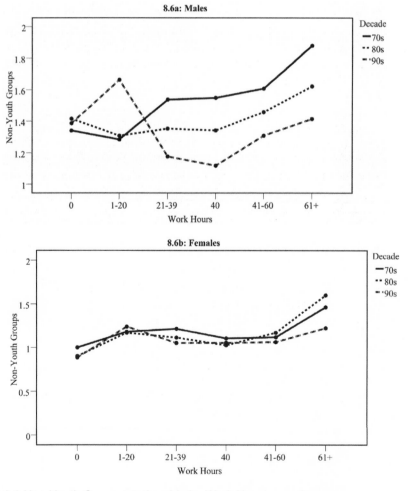

Figure 8.6 Non-Youth Group membership by Work Hours over time

The finding is so striking it is worth framing more precisely. In the first place, why break out the 1-20 category of work hours– containing only 6% of American workers—at all? One reason for not just collapsing 1-20 into a generic part-time category is *because* it differs so markedly from the 0 and 21-39 categories in its membership pattern; moreover, the percentage of workers in this category has grown each decade and still exceeds the 4.2% in the 61+ hours category. It is worth repeating that the rise in memberships in the low part-time worker category cannot be dismissed as some anomalous blip such as underemployed college grads floating to professional associations. Education, along with important factors sex and age, has been taken out of the picture by statistical control throughout these analyses. Further analyses (not shown) have indicated that the part-time peak is not the result of joining any one type of group; rather, it appears to be a more general associational pattern.[5] A final point to frame this finding concerns the other peak. The dots representing average memberships *always* rise after 40 hours, and the growth of more-than-full-time work is one of the strongest trends in the data.

Work and Social Networks

The analysis of close friends in Chapter 7 here (necessarily) switches to patterns of friendship socializing. To be succinct, there is not much of a pattern at all. Part-time workers seem to socialize a bit more, then additional hours make little discernible difference. But at every level of work, Americans in the 1990s spent more time with friends than they had in the 1970s. Generally, there has been no major change in the work-friendship (lack of a) pattern, but Americans do socialize with their friends more than they did in the Seventies regardless of hours.[6]

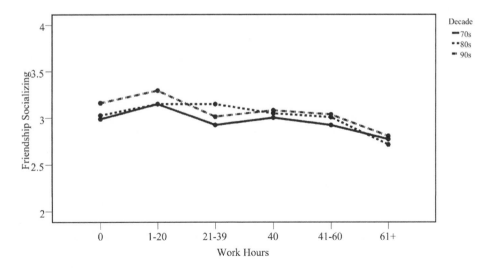

Figure 8.7 Friendship Socializing by Work Hours over time

Sex differences in Kin Socializing are well-known and well-observed in everyday American life, and are worthy of separate observation here. In female Figure 8.8b, the work-kin effect is remarkably flat and remarkably unchanged over time until the very highest levels of hours. Women working 61+ hours per week averaged the least Kin Socializing in the 1970s and 1980s, but the most in the 1990s (note the top dot at right). In male Figure 8.8a, it is helpful to look first at the most recent decade. The 1990s effect shows a curvilinear peak at 40 hours, gently sloping down to lesser Kin Socializing at the extremes of work. More importantly, the 1990s line is well below the 1970s line across the range of hours, thus indicating a downward shift in male socializing with kin. The visual evidence in Figures 8.8a and 8.8b is backed up by statistical evidence that Kin Socializing dropped at most levels of work for males—but not females—across the three decades.[7]

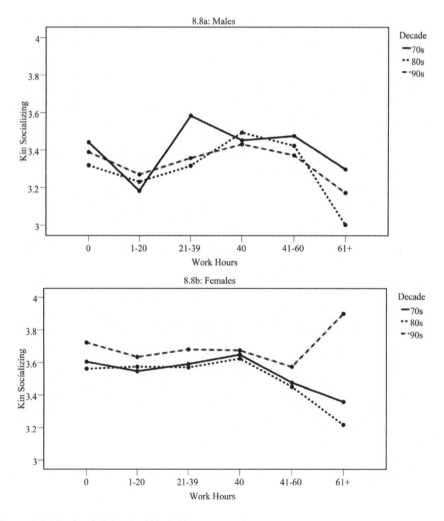

Figure 8.8 Kin Socializing by Work Hours over time

This is a noteworthy finding that needs to be reconciled with other data about relatives. First, Figure 7.10 in the previous chapter generally showed a positive tilt to the work-kin effect, such that both sexes in the highest hours category averaged about four visits a year more than non-workers. Recall that the item was phrased "…visited relatives in person or had them visit you"; contrast that wording with "How often do you spend a social evening with relatives" for the item behind Figure 8.8 here. As observed previously, the "spend a social evening" phrase connotes special occasions rather than simple "visits." It is speculation, but perhaps working more hours precludes additional dinner parties, but not dropping by for a pizza. Another related datum is drawn from Table 5.14a in Chapter 5. The male subtable there very nearly met the 5% rule-of-thumb standard for a drop in the high category of kin visits (the difference was 4.9%). The present Figure 8.8 projects the results of a more sophisticated statistical test that confirms the drop in male kin visiting.

Figure 8.9 requires few such complications. Although the analysis in Chapter 7 raised the issue of "the age-sensitivity of the work-neighboring relationship," a more basic fact here overwhelms all subsidiary findings about work and age: neighboring is down across the board. The track of the lines in the Figure does indicate that work reduces social evenings spent with neighbors, but the main action is the downward shift of the lines by decade.[8] The decline of neighboring in America pervades all ages, sexes, educational levels and, as is now apparent, levels of work as well.

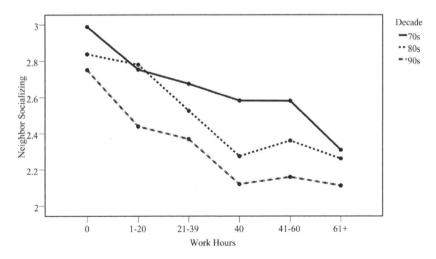

Figure 8.9 Neighbor Socializing by Work Hours over time

Family Structure and Social Networks

The current section in Chapter 7 found only a tenuous link between family and close friendships. Does that relationship hold for friendship socializing over time?

In Figure 8.10a, the answer is a resounding no. Regardless of decade, any investment at all in family life massively reduces "spending social evening(s)" with friends; the full investment of being married with children then incurs little further change. Notice that this dog-leg effect is similar by decade, but that the effect lines seem to be shifting upwards. So they are. The statistical tests confirm that friendship socializing across family statuses is rising decade by decade.[9]

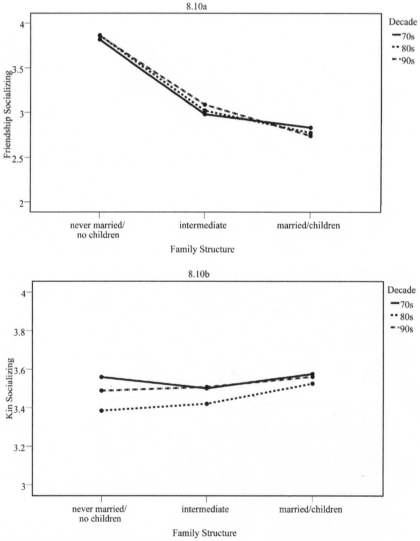

Figure 8.10 Network Socializing by Family Structure over time (*continued*)

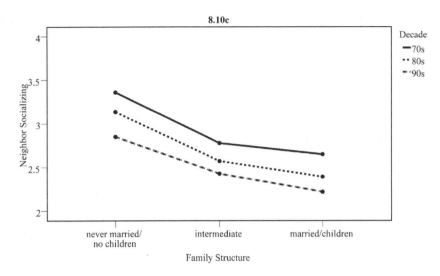

Figure 8.10 Network Socializing by Family Structure over time

Figure 8.10b likewise confirms findings from Chapter 7. Adding Family Structure also adds outside Kin Socializing, but here the lines do not follow a simple temporal sequence. The 1970s and 1990s lines are closer together, with a clear drop-off for the 1980s line.[10] Presently, the analysis will return to the matter of family dynamics by decade.

There is a departure from the Chapter 7 results in Figure 8.10c, but the reasons are well-known. "Spending a social evening" is hard enough for best friends, let alone neighbors, so here it declines with increasing family involvement. The line rose in Figure 7.13c of Chapter 7, it will be remembered, for "How often do you talk with or visit your immediate neighbors?" That statement sounds more like chatting in the driveway rather than having a block party, more of an everyday accompaniment of family life. The negative effect spotlighted here has two notable features. First, the lines are almost perfectly parallel as they decline with more family commitment. Second, there is a clear and substantial decade-to-decade decline in this kind of neighboring *regardless* of family commitment.[11]

Family Structure and Voluntary Association

The introduction to this section in Chapter 7 viewed the final arrow as the fault line in the disintegration of society. If America really is breaking down, the cracks should appear somewhere in the space between family and community. That previous inspection also turned up an unanticipated reinforcement structure. Specifically, age appears to increase the structural integrity of the family's support of voluntary association.

So Figure 8.11 retains the statistical controls for sex and education, but enters age directly into the analysis. The upgrade from the concluding figure of

Chapter 7, though, is that here the joint operation of family and age can be observed decade to decade. Visual inspection reveals a broad similarity across the decades for Americans married with children. In all three grids, the level of voluntary association shoots upward, then loses steam moving over to the 50+ dot. Americans with intermediate family commitments show a much more moderate ascension across the age range. Never married adults without children actually increased their group memberships across the lifespan in the Seventies (about half as much as those married with children), but by the Nineties their trend line had pitched downward. Despite the latter, relatively minor shift,[12] the conclusion of Chapter 7 can be accurately extended across these three decades: "It would appear that maturation means more community commitment the more family commitments one makes."[13]

The final finding of this chapter connects to three salient points. Point one: a formidable buttress continues to stabilize a key fault line in American society. The family-age stabilizer is subject to cross-stresses—as when shifts occur in

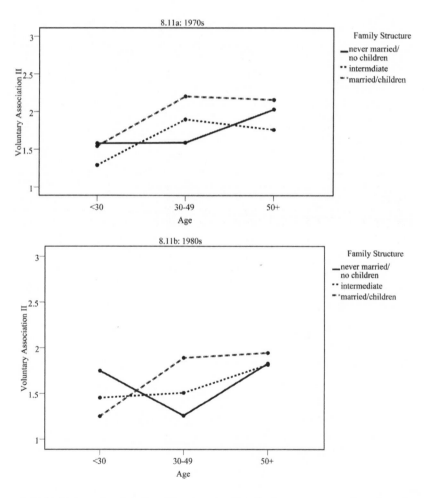

Figure 8.11 Voluntary Association II by Age for Family Structure over time (*continued*)

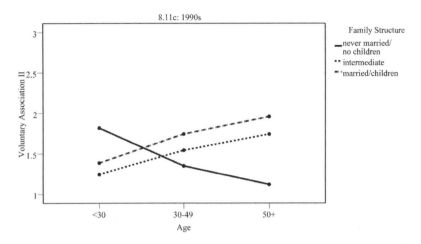

Figure 8.11 Voluntary Association II by Age for Family Structure over time

family life, a matter to be discussed at hand—but the buttress holds firm. Point two concerns Robert Putnam's argument in *Bowling Alone* that much of the decline of social commitment over the past generation is, in fact, generational. The "long civic generation" that weathered the Great Depression and World War II, he argues, were more socially involved than American cohorts before or since; hence, the erosion of social involvement as they have passed from the scene.[14] As has already been discussed in Chapter 6, it is easy to confuse age effects with cohort effects. What looks like a family-age interaction in Figure 7.15 could really just have been that the older folks also happened to be "long civic generation" married folks at survey time, and their unique civic ethos could be what really bumped up social involvement. Now it has been seen, however, that the family-age interaction shows no signs of waning. The family effect appears to be stable rather than a transient cohort effect. Salient point three is a point of departure. Now that the model of social capital has been built and time-tested, it can be used as a template to view *overall* trends across American society.

9

Social Capital and Social Inequality

CONCERNING OVERALL TRENDS

Social Capital

The entire weight of the model of social capital bears down on one-dimensional views of trends. Whatever credence one assigns to the empirical evidence supporting each model arrow, there is little serious question that the four types of social capital are interconnected. This fact makes it problematical to do an accounting of, say, voluntary association while pretending that work, family and social networks do not figure into the account. Not only is the data indisputable that they *do* figure in, but they have also changed significantly over this accounting period.

All of these considerations sound warnings klaxons when approaching "overall trends" in social capital. The analysis here will exercise the appropriate caution by dutifully following a three-step procedure. First, changes in each capital component are to be viewed through the familiar MANOVA routine using decade as the explanatory variable; this will highlight the direction of change (if any) while washing out year-to-year fluctuations that may mask trends. The second step is to properly incorporate the control variables that have been featured throughout the previous chapters. Charting simple changes in hours worked from the 70s through the 90s without taking account of the revolution in female careerism over this period would be, well, too simplistic. Likewise, the more moderate downward shift in investments in family life among older than younger Americans means that a statistical adjustment for age needs to be made. Third, interpretations of these carefully calibrated changes in each form of social capital will be illuminated by other evidence from the model already on the record. For instance, a flat line indicating no change in kin interaction is cast in an entirely different light if people are de-investing in family life (which they are) than if family investments are stable (which they are not).

Social Inequality

The linkage of social capital to social inequality—the little "and" in this chapter's title—has been recognized from the very start. In the first sentence of his introduction to Democracy in America, Tocqueville declaims, "No NOVELTY in the United States struck me more vividly during my stay there than the equality of conditions."[1] John Ehrenberg's essay "Equality, Democracy and Community" states that Tocqueville's work shows that "...community social capital and civil society require economic equality."[2]

Many contemporary analysts are struck by the significance of this linkage. Putnam puts it particularly strongly: "...the correlation between economic equality and social capital is virtually ubiquitous, both across space and across time, both in the United States and around the world."[3] Nevertheless, inequality issues receive short shrift in many current assessments of social capital in America; in *Bowling Alone*, Putnam "...explicitly denies that historic levels of economic inequality play an important role."[4] This is puzzling, especially given that the widening class separations in American society over the past thirty years are a point of consensus across the social sciences.

Education and Race

In the analyses to immediately follow, shifts in social capital will be viewed directly through the prisms of education and race. This is a particularly powerful way to turn up the magnification on overall trends for three major reasons. First of all, it permits the identification of the *separate* effects of these two aspects of inequality. Numerous findings in previous chapters were clouded by the confounding of education with race—black/white differences in voluntary association might be driven by black/white differences in education, for example. Second, MANOVA tests for statistical interaction could highlight the *combined* effects of education and race. Is it not possible—in fact, plausible—that education might intensify race differences in social network patterns? Third and finally, the foregrounding of these particular aspects of inequality is highly recommended since they *themselves* have been the sites of mighty social changes over the relevant period. Salient race-specific shifts that have been well-observed include deepening poverty in deprived communities and the rise of the black middle class.[5] The latter phenomenon, of course, has been propelled by the "virtual explosion" in America's college enrollment already documented above (in Table 6.18).[6] As the premiere variable for raising social capital, the level of education in America needs to be seen right in front of overall trends.

ANALYSES OF OVERALL TRENDS

Work

Chapter 3 has nicely set the stage for the somewhat more complex production of Figure 9.1. Work hours are up across the board, but especially so for women and the middle-aged; these well-understood differentials justify entering sex and age into the MANOVA as background control variables (technically, as "covariates"). Hours on the job have accelerated faster at higher levels of education, and at comparable rates for blacks and whites. Both education and race are on direct display as markers of social inequality in Figure 9.1.

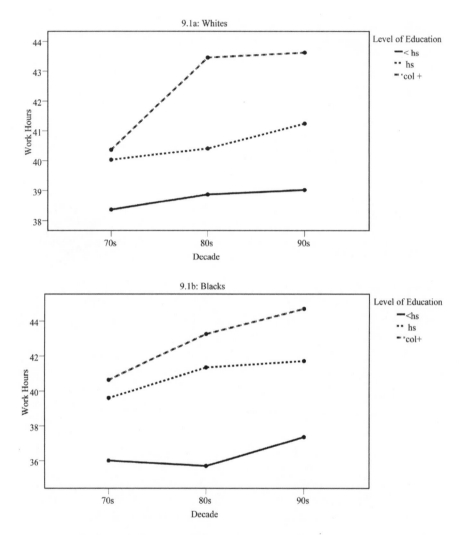

Figure 9.1 Work Hours by Decade for level of education by Race

Note immediately the general upward sweep of the lines. This, of course, bespeaks the general increase in work effort in the American population, but some differences are apparent. In both the white and black panels, each higher line seems to elevate a bit more from the 1970s through the 1990s. What this suggests is an intensification of the trend towards more work at each higher level of education. This is, in fact, a nice definition of an interaction effect, which the statistical test bears out.[7] So: for Americans of both races, folks with more education added more work hours over the past thirty years.

Family

While a more finely textured breakdown of changes in family status is presented in Chapter 4, for the present purposes of global analysis the Family Structure variable is to be employed. It will be recalled that it is scored zero for no marriage and no children, two for currently married with children, and one for everybody else (intermediate).

As the dependent variable in Figure 9.2, it is clear that Family Structure in America has been in decline. All six lines do descend from the 1970s to the 1980s, regardless of level of education. From the 1980s to the 1990s, though, the less than high school and high school lines continue their descent and both college lines do not. In fact, for both black and white college respondents, family investments actually creep up a bit over the last decade.

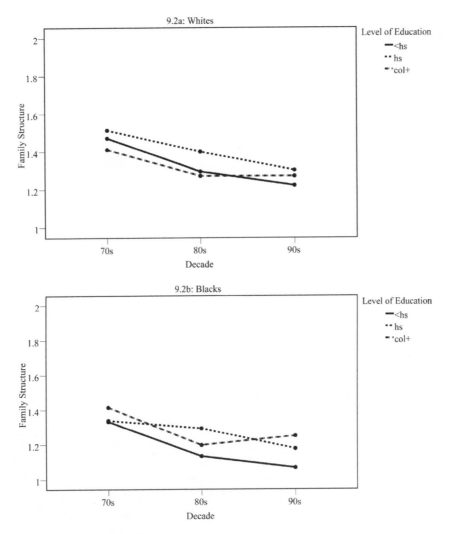

Figure 9.2 Family Structure by Decade for level of education by Race

This is consistent with the simple tabular findings in Chapter 4 that family life has slipped the least for college level Americans, but the present result is more sophisticated because of the statistical controls that yield a "purer" effect for both education and race. The nature of that (improved) effect is, again, a statistical interaction.[8] College respondents have de-invested in family significantly less than respondents with lesser education levels. Moreover, this difference is robust across the races. Even though black Americans generally have lower scores than whites in Family Structure, the college reversal from the 80s to the 90s is still clearly there.

Social Networks

In the aggregate, are Americans weakening their social bonds with other Americans? The answer in Chapter 5 is multi-faceted, but pretty neatly summarized by the visuals in the lower right-hand box at the beginning of Chapter 8. As measured by the "spend a social evening" frequency of socializing, neighboring is way down, hanging out with friends is up a bit, and kin interaction is pretty steady (despite the decline of family life).

But the real issue here involves the phrase "in the aggregate." The decline of any single type of social relationship would be of more concern to greeting card companies than to pundits of social capital. Figure 9.3 displays changes in Informal Socializing, which adds up the "spend a social evening" items for kin, neighbors and friends to yield an aggregate measure of network contact.

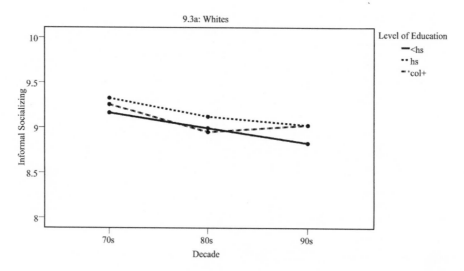

Figure 9.3 Informal Socializing by Decade for level of education by Race (*continued*)

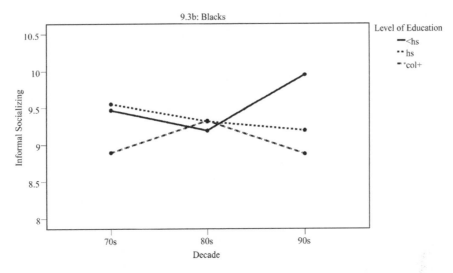

Figure 9.3 Informal Socializing by Decade for level of education by Race

In the Figure, overall socializing drops for all three educational levels of white Americans. That slide seems to stop for college respondents in the 1990s, which parallels the stabilization of family life seen in Figure 9.2. The education paths for black Americans in Figure 9.3b are very different and much less readily interpretable.[9] College respondents surge in socializing during the 80s, then tail off in the 90s. Less than high schoolers pretty much do the opposite, dropping then rising to above their starting level. Only high school graduates show a steady decline across the three decades.

This is a crucial point in the analysis. Instead of just reproducing the analytical framework for each form of social capital and then attempting to make sense of each Figure on its face, it is important to seek other sources of illumination. One such source of light has already been shed elsewhere by the model. It is well documented in Chapter 5 that "spend a social evening" neighboring has plummeted widely and deeply in America, which is *not* the case for kin and friend socializing. This means that most of the downward push on any line in Figure 9.3 is highly neighbor-specific. Also well-documented is a slight but sustained upward push in friend socializing for many categories of respondents. Rather than a general weakening of social bonds in America, there appears to be a gradual replacement of people who happen to live nearby—neighbors—with people more to one's own choosing—friends.

Voluntary Association

Another source of illumination is simplification. Figure 9.4 strips down the analytical model to the simplest of trends in Voluntary Association II with no other variable at all. In fact, it is a non-trend. Average group memberships actually do not change significantly in America at all across this period.[10] This would seem

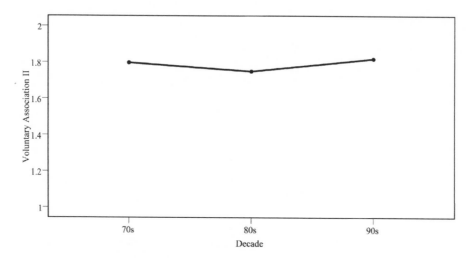

Figure 9.4 Voluntary Association II by Decade

to belie Chapter 6, which did find some substantial declines in voluntary association, especially within educational levels.

That is a key clue. Figure 9.5 restores the familiar variables to the MANO-
VA model, and behold: all six lines do tilt downward across the decades, signifying a significant change.[11] Before attempting to reconcile Figures 9.4 and 9.5,
observe the large distances that separate the lines from each other within each
panel. This is just another manifestation of the huge capital-accumulating impact
education has on voluntary association. So group memberships may be sliding a
bit *inside* each educational level, but Americans are *climbing* those levels so fast
that the net trend is virtually nil.

A close comparison of panels 9.5a and 9.5b seems to show a steeper decli-
nation of the lines for black Americans and, in fact, the statistical test bears that
out.[12] In the interest of further simplification, the analysis separately examined
each of the sixteen constituent groups of Voluntary Association II. "Labor unions" and "church-affiliated" groups sustained the most significant declines, and
especially so for black respondents.[13] Now consider real racial differences. Black
Americans are more heavily represented in working-class occupations—
especially manufacturing—that have been rapidly disappearing along with their
unions. Black Americans generally have higher levels of religious affiliation
than do white Americans, even with the recent declines. Given these differences,
what is the proper interpretation of the course of voluntary association in American society?

Perhaps the final source of illumination should come from historical context. The "de-industrialization"—and, hence, "de-unionization"—of America
has been highlighted recently due to globalization, but it is really part of the
conversion to a service economy which had been gradually occurring for the
better part of the 20th century.[14] Secularization—broadly defined as the decline of

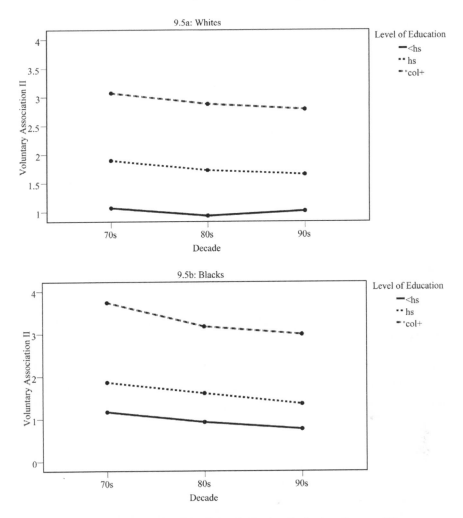

Figure 9.5 Voluntary Association II by Decade for level of education and Race

religious commitment—is considered a pervasive trend sweeping across modern societies everywhere.[15] So the primary sources of dropping voluntary association from the 1970s to the 1990s are themselves part of primary historical processes.[16] If unions and church groups are excluded from the list, Americans actually have *increased* their voluntary associations over recent history.

POSTSCRIPT: DIFFERENTIAL RETURNS TO SOCIAL CAPITAL

The routine inclusion of race and education together in the above series of analyses has been the source of a further surprise. There is a well-established literature in economics and sociology documenting the "differential returns" to human capital inputs.[17] In a nutshell, the research shows that whites average higher earnings than do blacks at a given level of education. Years of schooling is viewed as an investment for which white Americans receive better "bang for the (human capital) buck."

In reviewing the coefficients for the MANOVAs in the present chapter, an untargeted effect kept hitting the mark. Race and education *together* repeatedly connected with the many forms of social capital. This set of findings was unanticipated, but it resonates with the rationale to consider the "combined" effects of our two measures of inequality as described in the Education and Race section above.

Figure 9.6 displays a simple result. The steeper slope of the line for black Americans means that they benefit more from additional years of schooling in terms of added work hours. A significant race-education interaction backs up this observation.[18]

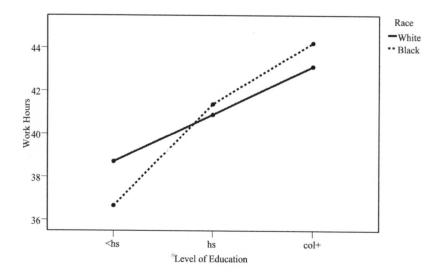

Figure 9.6 Work Hours by Level of Education by Race

In Figure 9.7 Family Structure is the targeted form of social capital. The line declines for white college respondents, but not at all for blacks. The MANOVA test for the interaction effect bears out this racial difference: more education is more negatively associated with family investment for white than black Americans.[19]

Using the combined measure of Informal Socializing in Figure 9.8, the racial contrast reverses direction. Here white folks who have finished high school clearly have more active social lives than those who have not, but there is little additional benefit of having gone to college. Black folks get some social benefit from a high school degree (they are the most socially active of all Americans), but college is associated with a bit less association. This racial difference is also statistically significant.[20]

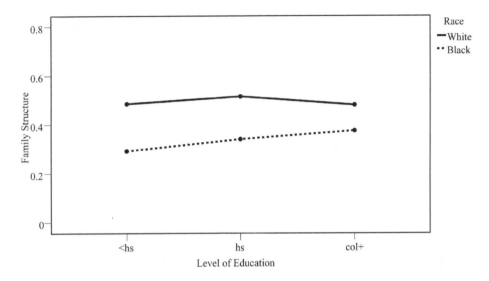

Figure 9.7 Family Structure by Level of Education by Race

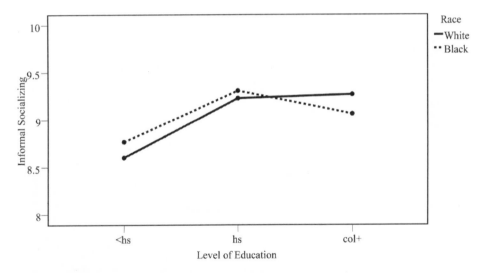

Figure 9.8 Informal Socializing by Level of Education by Race

In the final panel of Figure 9.9, Voluntary Association II is on display, and its most striking feature is the steepness of both lines. The statistically significant race-education effect turns up for the fourth figure in a row, and one can readily discern that black Americans' averages finish higher than whites' at the college level. However, the raw power of education over voluntary association dwarfs the race interaction.[21]

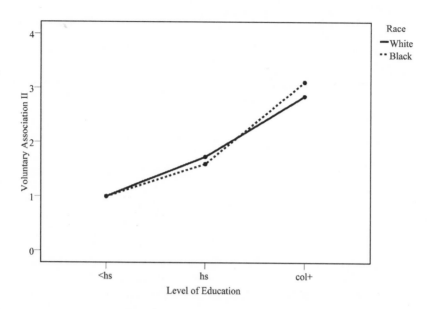

Figure 9.9 Voluntary Association II by Level of Education by Race

There are three reasons to call this section's results "surprising." First, they were discovered while crunching the numbers in search of "overall trends." Second, these findings (with one exception) actually reverse those of the differential returns to human capital literature. Black Americans actually get more social capital than white Americans for each degree deposited. Third and finally, they justify with an unexpected flourish this two-barreled approach to relate social capital to social inequality. It is a partial realization of the promise foreseen by researchers such as Grace Kao of the University of Pennsylvania: "With greater precision in its definition, social capital (and its components) can serve as powerful tool for understanding educational stratification by race…"[22]

10

Social Capital Futures

> In national surveys conducted in recent
> years three out of four parents say they
> fear that their child will be kidnapped
> by a stranger. They harbor this anxiety,
> no doubt, because they keep hearing
> frightening statistics and stories about
> perverts snatching children off the
> street... John Walsh, father of Adam
> Walsh, whose abduction and murder at a
> shopping mall in Hollywood, Florida,
> got the country focused on missing
> children in the first place, proclaimed
> the country 'littered with mutilated, de-
> capitated, raped, and strangled child-
> ren.'[1]
> —*Barry Glassner,*
> *The Culture of Fear*

SOCIAL CAPITAL IMAGES AND ISSUES

Missing children was one of the suddenly sensational issues of 1980s America.
The glare of the media spotlight on the Walsh and other cases produced, in effect, a brand new social problem in the public mind. The horrifying nature of
these stories was reinforced by startling statistics claiming that up to 800,000
children went missing every year in the U.S. The expert estimate of only 200-
300 children per year rarely made it into dramatic TV or newspaper accounts.[2]
As a result, there was a surge in national concern about "stranger danger," and
millions of haunted parents.

In 1990s America, school shootings made a similar media splash:

> Banner headlines and terrifying photos screamed from the front pages of the
> nation's dailies. Round-the-clock television coverage broadcast images of dis-
> traught teenagers huddled in the hallways, anguished parents weeping behind
> police lines, ambulance gurneys wheeling the dead and injured from play-
> grounds to emergency rooms, and grave stones rising.[3]

These images are still raw and fresh in people's minds, and filed into a whole new category of social problems. Gruesome tales aside, school shootings have been subjected to social scientific analysis, notably a study commissioned by the U.S. Department of Education and the National Academy of Sciences. The resultant book, *Rampage: The Social Roots of School Shootings* by Katherine S. Newman of Harvard's Kennedy School of Government, is full of intriguing findings. In the first place, "rampage" shootings did increase in the Nineties; however, the rise of this specific form of school violence—to an average of about one "rampage" a year—happened during a decade when general youth homicide and school violence *dropped* nationwide.[4] And rampage shootings are a small fraction of the carnage committed in inner-city slum schools in any given year. But the school shootings in Newman's study have famously happened out of the slums that fit the public image of violent areas, and that is just where *Social Capital in America* comes in.

Experts on social problems often cite the power of *expectations* to plant issues in the public mind.[5] Stories that shock and appall do so precisely because they are not supposed to happen, or, more to the point, because they "are not supposed to happen HERE." The latter quote is a staple of local news interviews with shaken neighbors after a tragedy, and it has immediate relevance. Hollywood, Florida is an affluent new suburb; the Columbine community is equally favored and equally white. Of course, everybody knows that there is epidemic violence in Watts and the Bronx, but that is just where the public expects it to be. Americans had no expectations of automatic weapons rampages in Ferris Buehler's hood. Hence, the 10,000 stories in the nation's leading papers post-Columbine,[6] and the growing sense that something evil is loose in America's schools and the communities in which they are set.

The sense of impending evil recalls Chapter 1. The title "What Is *Wrong* with People?" prefaced public opinion polls showing that Americans are not only worried about particular social issues, but deeply concerned that something is rotten at the core of America. Snatched suburban children and "Matrix" movie scenes in affluent schools have led people to believe that, in our terms, social capital has been lost. This is a good reason to perform hard sociological analysis to see if it is so, but there is another connection to the present subject. Concern about social capital must also be reconciled with its complexity. Katherine Newman's analysis in *Rampage* focused on Heath, Kentucky and Westside, Arkansas—both sites of school shootings, and both rural small towns. These communities, she found, were literally bursting with traditional social capital:

> Outside of small-town USA, the decline of social capital and the corresponding longing for the resurrection of community has been a powerful narrative …But this decline and fall story, powerful as it is, cannot account for the tragedies in Heath and Westside. [Robert] Putnam would find much to admire in both places, for they epitomize the kind of America he is searching for. Parents of Heath High School students are very involved in their children's lives and activities. Nobody locks their doors in the Westside area, because the neighbors have known each other for generations…Heath and Westside are the exceptions that prove Putnam's rule, or so they thought.[7]

In fact, Newman's research revealed that "the very density of community structure" in small towns can contribute to such shootings. One of the mayors remarked, "This place is just like Mayberry"; Newman's data show that 60% of rampage shootings have happened in prototypical small towns over the past 30 years.[8] The point is not that stranger snatchings and school rampages disprove the relevance of social capital. On the contrary, Newman documents enormous benefits of vibrant groups and social networks for these communities. What is crucial, rather, is to recognize the complexity of social capital. Neither social problems nor social benefits can be inferred by simple matters of amount. As we have seen in detail, the types of social capital link to each other in intricate ways. Looking at only one type at a time so simplifies things as to be silly; looking at all types together without care for the pattern can lead to mistakes like those resolved in *Rampage*.

These are important caution signs for the present analysis in projecting trend lines into the future. It will do so in two steps. Step one will address the matter of media technology—specifically, television and the computer—and its prospects for social capital in America. The temptation is to treat these pieces of hardware as outside agents of change which either raise or lower the level of such capital. Ferocious debates in academic journals and the public press reflect such simplistic positions. That temptation will be resisted here by using the model that has been built and tested as a template for media effects. The second and final step will be to summarize developments within this model as augurs for the future of social capital in America.

MEDIA TECHNOLOGY AND SOCIAL CAPITAL

Television

> When the history of the twentieth century is written with greater perspective than we now enjoy, the impact of technology on communications and leisure will almost certainly be a major theme.[9]
>
> —*Robert D. Putnam,*
> *Bowling Alone*

So begins Putnam's case for television as a major culprit in the killing of social capital in America. There is *prima facie* evidence to support this accusation, but it is certainly not an open-and-shut case. Elsewhere in the chapter that is the source of the above quote, Putnam observes that "...the astounding series of poor predictions about the social consequences of the telephone is a deeply cautionary tale."[10] Caution is to be exercised here by sticking to a basic rule of evidence: cross-examine television from *within* the model of social capital. Tossing out education, work and family by ignoring or statistically controlling them is like tossing out the testimony of co-conspirators.

Figure 10.1 displays Voluntary Association by level of TV viewing for each level of education. Clearly, more TV viewership is associated with less group membership, as indicated by the downward tilt of all three lines to the right.

Even clearer, though, is the size of the separation between the lines. In statistical terms, education is over thirteen times as powerful in inflating Voluntary Association as television is in deflating it.[11] Figure 10.2 performs the same operation for Informal Socializing with weaker results. The downward tug of TV watching on network interaction is barely perceptible, but the upward push of education is unmistakable.[12] Even accepting for the moment that TV watching does erode both Voluntary Association and Informal Socializing, the rapidly rising educational levels in the U.S. would seem to be a much more powerful countertrend building them back up. Besides, more educated folks tend to watch less television.[13]

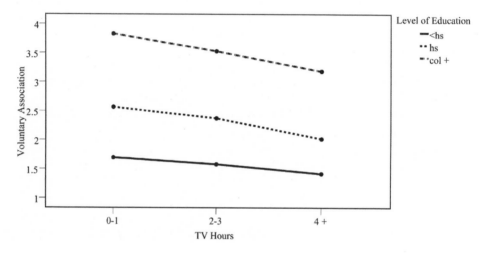

Figure 10.1 Voluntary Association by TV Hours for level of education

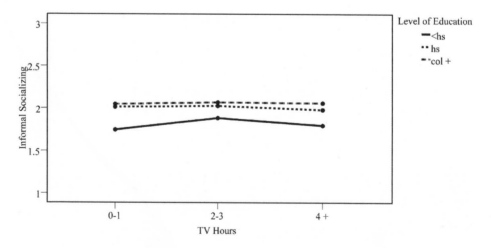

Figure 10.2 Informal Socializing by TV Hours for level of education

Now that the most important control variable has been incorporated into the analysis of television effects, it is time to provide the context of the model of social capital itself. Figure 10.3 reviews the TV-Voluntary Association connection through the primary responsibilities of work and family, respectively. That connection is apparent in Figure 10.3a; Americans who watch 4 or more hours of TV a day belong to almost a full group less, on average, than Americans who watch only 0-1 hour. Nevertheless, work is the more powerful variable affecting voluntary association.[14] The relative height of the lines is also notable. Americans working the most fill out the top line, part-timers the middle and, as observed before, 40-hours-a-week workers have the lowest membership across the board. Turning immediately to Figure 10.3b, both television and Family Structure exert comparable effects on group membership, although the drop-off of Voluntary Association at the highest level of TV viewership is especially pronounced among married Americans with kids.[15]

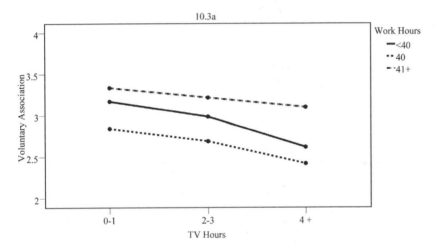

Figure 10.3a Voluntary Association by TV Hours for level of work hours

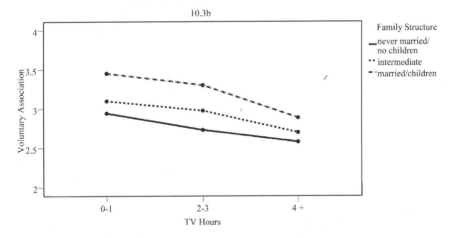

Figure 10.3b Voluntary Association by TV Hours for level of family structure

Figure 10.3 is full of interpretable findings, but the concern here is to focus upon their significance within the social capital model. Putnam's concern is that Americans across the board are, in effect, cutting the PTA meeting to stay home and watch "The Simpsons." If true, this means TV is driving out social capital, which does fit the data pattern in Figure 10.3. Also consistent within the data, however, is a mental picture that has people deciding not to go to the meeting, then flicking on "The Simpsons" for something to do; if this is the true picture, the causal arrow goes *from* social capital decisions *to* TV as a time filler rather than a time stealer. At this point, the evidence for either case is pretty circumstantial.[16]

In advance of a special study (which would probably have to analyze a cohort sample over time) to settle this question, three points provide the proper perspective. First of all, the TV-as-a-cause theory can only apply to the right side of the social capital model; nobody seriously contends that people are turning down marriage proposals or work hours so they can watch more television. Secondly, notice that the top two lines in Figure 10.3a represent growing segments of the workforce. Americans working more than full time are both more common and more likely to participate in groups; the 1-20 hours category within the middle line is expanding, too, and has become increasingly group-centric as shown in Chapter 8. So even if all of the downward tilt in the lines really is people passing up meetings to free up Prime Time, these work trends will still exert upward pressure on aggregate membership in the USA. Point three is circumstantial evidence in the other direction: television watching is not increasing. According to the GSS, average hours of TV watched by Americans was actually a bit *lower* in the Nineties than in the Seventies.[17]

Taking a tip from Chapter 9, Figure 10.4 spotlights a familiar feature of social networks using the race-education level breakdown. While there is some

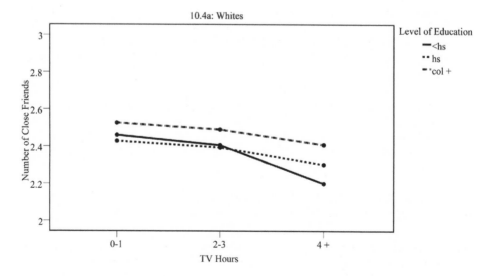

Figure 10.4 Number of Close Friends by TV Hours for level of education by race (*continued*)

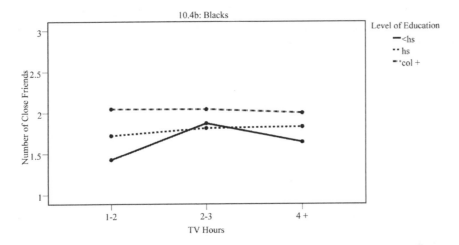

Figure 10.4 Number of Close Friends by TV Hours for level of education by race

slippage in number of close friends reported by heavy-watching white respondents, such is not the case for black respondents. Two of the three lines for the latter are higher to the right, and for college black Americans the line is almost perfectly flat.[18] Nor is this an isolated finding for social networks. TV watching is actually positively associated with neighbor socializing for *all* races and education levels (not shown). Clearly, the social capital effects of the small screen bear closer scrutiny.

The Internet

There is, of course, another "small screen" that is the subject of the national discussion on social capital. The personal computer is the electronic doorway to a realm whose very name, internet, suggests a constituent social structure. The immediate question is what this new form of media technology means for other, more traditional forms of social structure. Or, as Putnam puts it,

> Will the Internet in practice turn out to be a niftier telephone or a niftier television? In other words, will the Internet become predominantly a means of active, social communication or a means of private, passive entertainment? Will computer-mediated communication "crowd out" face-to-face ties? It is, in this domain especially, much too early to know.[19]

Perhaps not. Putnam's SCCBS dataset (gathered after *Bowling Alone* was published) permits a parallel analysis to that just performed for television. Figure 10.5 arrays responses to, "How many hours do you spend on the Internet in a typical week?" in increasing order from none to 6+ hours. The contrast with television could hardly be more striking. WWW-time is *positively* associated with Voluntary Association, and the steep upward slopes indicate a *lot* more association. Intriguingly, Americans without a high school degree gain the most, almost doubling their group memberships across these extremes of internet time; even college graduates, who already tower above less educated respondents in terms of overall membership, gain an average of half a group from left to right.[20] Informal Socializing is addressed in Figure 10.6, which tells a watered-down version of the same story. More internet time means more rather than less face-to-face time, and especially so for the least educated Americans.[21]

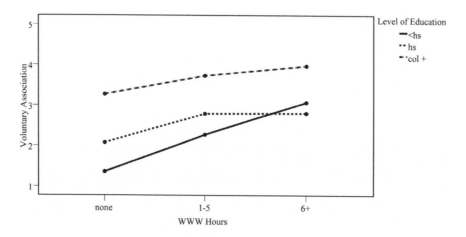

Figure 10.5 Voluntary Association by WWW Hours for level of education

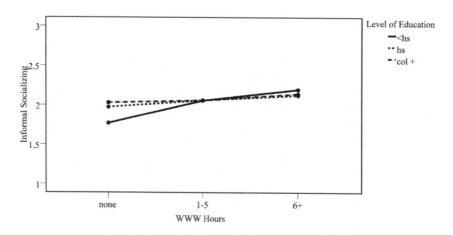

Figure 10.6 Informal Socializing by WWW Hours for level of education

Figure 10.7 again drops the social capital model across the analysis as a template through which to view media effects. Two broad patterns are apparent across all levels of work hours and family commitment. First, internet involvement *always* means a higher average level of Voluntary Association; the right-hand dot is above the left-hand dot in every single subset of work or family capital. Second, most of the step-up happens at the first step: virtually all lines rise most steeply at the transition between unwired (none) and wired (1 to 5 hours). This might mean that higher levels of internet usage manifest different effects than getting wired in the first place, but breaking that possibility down will have to await future analyses. For now, there is simply no question that being on the internet is positively compatible with Voluntary Association.[22]

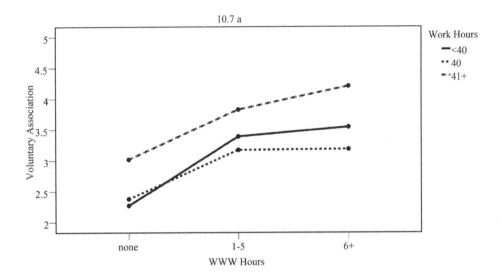

Figure 10.7a Voluntary Association by WWW Hours for level of work hours

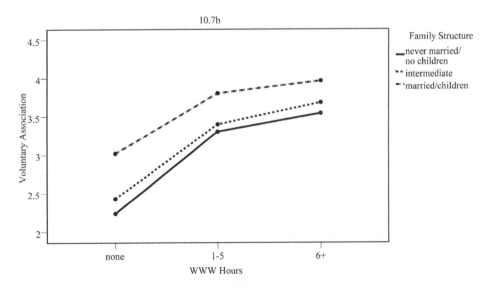

Figure 10.7b Voluntary Association by WWW Hours for level of family structure

SOCIAL CAPITAL IN AMERICA

The State of the Model

Before addressing the value of the findings it has generated, the most important thing to say about the model of social capital is this: *it is a model*. Pundits too numerous to mention (although many were mentioned in Chapters 1 and 2) have decried the lack of conceptual clarity in this field. Investigators often myopically limit the view to a highly specialized subarea—like family and academic achievement, for example—or dizzingly expand the view to encompass any noun after the adjective "social." The model in play here has attempted to assay the main varieties of social capital in a coherent way.

Has it succeeded? To extend the titular metaphor, each of the four major forms of social capital has been firmly "grounded" in both classical and contemporary theory. Moreover, each has been applied by multiple researchers in multiple disciplines. But the present work was never meant to be an exercise in pedantic scholarship. Piling up stacks of learned citations to support a model is an empty kind of proof. Essentially, Chapter 2 argued that all of its intellectual grounding was meant to establish a *prima facie* case for the model. The real test would be in the quality of the data it could pull out of the ground. On that score, the haul has been quite handsome. The General Patterns tables in Chapters 3 through 6 revealed major differences in capital accounts by sex, age, race and, especially, education; the latter variables were also sites of differential change across the time period spanning Societal Trends. Perhaps the most persuasive evidence for the integrity of the model was laid out in Chapter 7. One may quibble about their precise texture, but there can be little serious question about the density of the interconnections among the four forms of social capital. What makes a model a model is precisely that its various parts are too tightly linked to be overlooked. One may ignore the effects of family upon voluntary association, but one will be ignoring something essential.

One way to look at Chapter 8 is as an extended test of the social capital model. Each effect line was reproduced decade by decade to check for shifts in the nature of the linkages. There have been such shifts, certainly, but none that markedly modify the interrelationships. Investments in family structure increased kin socializing and reduced friend socializing in the 1970s. Such was still the case in the 1990s.

After eight chapters of preliminary—but absolutely necessary—analysis, Chapter 9 finally got down to the question of overall trends with the full model up and running. An additional—also necessary—modification was to build race and education directly into the analysis as measures of inequality. The logic behind this final step stretches back to Tocqueville himself, who had linked America's voluntary association to its very un-Francelike equality. This old idea paid rich current dividends. For both black and whites, more education (as a measure of class inequality) converted into more of an increase in work commitment over time. Family commitment declined for both races, but college braked the rate of its decline. Voluntary association has dwindled somewhat within educational levels, but the latter so powerfully expands the former that Americans scrambling up the school ladder have cancelled out any aggregate drop. The education/race results for informal socializing are a bit less clear for the "spend a social evening" GSS items, but is worth returning to the simpler findings of Chapter 5. When socializing is defined as number of visits—as it is in the SCCBS—education is their most powerful elevator. The rising educational levels of Americans therefore will have been lifting the level of informal visiting as well.

The Future of the Model

The analyses of media technology in this chapter light a clear path for extending the conceptual framework of *Social Capital in America*. Using hours of use of TV or the internet as an explanatory variable is using a dull dissection knife indeed. Clearly, what is *on* those visual screens does matter. Watching TV news has been strongly linked to social involvement; watching "The Simpsons" has not. Organizing a neighborhood association online is a social capital creation; visiting pornsites is not.

The need to delve into media content suggests a more fundamental metamorphosis of the model. Quite simply, the foregoing analysis has not delved into the minds of Americans. Except for perusing polls about Americans' fear of societal breakdown, the model has stuck to the hard, shiny material of the buried treasures themselves. This was deliberate. Work, family, voluntary association and social networks are big subjects about which too little was—and still is—known. But an exclusive focus on social structure imposes intellectual limits. Now that the model has been laid out and trends have been traced, what does it all mean?

Pursuing meaning is a matter of getting inside peoples' heads. Hours on the job are on the rise, but is this accompanied by job satisfaction or job stress? Figuring out why Americans who work 60 hours a week join so many groups must be rooted in personal motivations; what are they? Or consider education, which has been colorfully referred to as the "philosopher's stone" of social capital. That is a reference to medieval alchemists' notion that this object could magically transform base metals into gold. Given the treasure image here, it is an apt metaphor. To move beyond the metaphorical, education's pervasive power requires scientific explanation. How does finishing college at age 21 produce more association in people's lives at age 50? Answers to such questions should be sought in the value Americans themselves assign to the social capital in their lives.

NOTES

CHAPTER 1

1. Michael Zuckerman, *Peaceable Kingdoms: New England Towns in the Eighteenth Century* (Alfred A. Knopf, 1970).

2. Daniel Yankelovich, "Trends in American Cultural Values," *Criterion 35*, no. 3 (Autumn 1996), 2-9. It is notable that Yankelovich's documentation of public distress occurred at about the same time as this article first appeared and created a bit of a sensation: Robert D. Putnam, "Bowling Alone: America's Declining Social Capital," *Journal of Democracy* 6:1 (January, 1995), 65-78.

3. CNN/*USA Today*/Gallup poll, May 9-12, 1996.

4. Chilton Research Services, "Real National Unease—Especially on the 'Moral Dimension,'" *The Public Perspective* (October-November 1996), 24.

5. NBC News/*Wall Street Journal* Poll conducted by Peter Hart and Robert Teeter, June 16-19, 1999.

6. Public Agenda, "Kids These Days '99: What Americans Really Think about the Next Generation" (Public Agenda Report, 1999), 1-10.

7. Cited in Lisa Ferraro Parmelee, "Faces of Youth," *The Public Perspective* (January/February 2002), 19.

8. C. Wright Mills, *The Sociological Imagination* (Oxford University Press, 1956).

9. Pew Research Center, "Motherhood Today," May 9, 1997.

10. CNN/*USA Today*/Gallup poll, op. cit.; Gallup, "Satisfaction with the United States, 1979-2009" (http://www.gallup.com/poll/1669/General-Mood-Country.aspx).

11. Charles Derber, *The Wilding of America: How Greed and Violence are Eroding our Nation's Character* (St. Martin's Press, 1996); Frank Hearn, *Moral Order and Social Disorder: The American Search for Civil Society* (Aldine de Gruyter, 1997); Richard Sennett, *The Corrosion of Character* (W. W. Norton, 1998); John A. Hall and Charles Lindholm, *Is America Breaking Apart?* (Princeton University Press, 1999); Robert Bork, *Slouching Toward Gomorrah* (Regan Books, 1996).

12. Putnam, "Bowling Alone: America's Declining Social Capital," op. cit.; Robert D. Putnam, *Bowling Alone: The Collapse and Revival of American Community* (Simon & Schuster, 2000).

13. Everett C. Ladd, "A Vast Empirical Record Refutes the Idea of Civic Deline," *The Public Perspective* (June/July 1996), 1-35.

14. Council on Civil Society, "A Call to Civil Society: Why Democracy Needs Moral Truths," Pamphlet (Institute for American Values, 1999), 3.

15. Penn National Commission on Society, Culture and Community, http://www.upenn.edu/pnc/public.html (2002), 2.

16. Michael Schudson, *The Good Citizen: A History of American Civic Life* (The Free Press, 1998), 301.

17. Mark Buchanan, *Nexus: Small Worlds and the Groundbreaking Science of Networks* (W. W. Norton & Company, 2002), 143.

18. James Allan Davis and Tom W. Smith: General Social Surveys, 1972-2000. [machine-readable data file]. Principal Investigator, James A. Davis; Director and Co-Principal Investigator, Tom W. Smith; Co-Principal Investigator, Peter V. Marsden, NORC ed. Chicago: National Opinion Research Center, producer, 2005; Storrs, CT: The

Roper Center for Public Opinion and Research, University of Connecticut, distributor. 1 data file (51,020 logical records) and 1 codebook (2,552 pp).

19. Saguaro Seminar at John F. Kennedy School of Government, Harvard University, *Social Capital Benchmark Survey, 2000*. TNS Interresearch, producer; Storrs, CT: The Roper Center for Public Opinion Research, University of Connecticut, distributor. 1 data file (29,733 logical records). For the analyses below, the 41 community studies have been aggregated with the national sample to produce an overall sample size of n • 30,000. This produces much greater statistical power for the multivariate comparisons and is technically sound since "… extensive analysis has failed to unearth any significant differences between the nationally representative sample of 3,000 and the aggregate of the 41 local sites (n = 27,000), either in frequency distributions or in relations among variables." See Robert D. Putnam, "*E Pluribus Unum*: Diversity and Community in the Twenty-first Century—The 2006 Johan Skytte Prize Lecture, *Scandinavian Political Studies* (Vol. 30, No. 2), 166.

CHAPTER 2

1. Alexis de Tocqueville, *Democracy in America*, Vol. 2 (Random House, 1990), 106.

2. James S. Coleman, "Social Capital in the Creation of Human Capital" in *Social Capital: A Multifaceted Perspective*, edited by Partha Dasgupta and Ismail Serageldin (World Bank, 2000), 16. In *Bowling Alone*, Putnam contends that the term has been "…independently invented at least six times over in the twentieth century" (19).

3. David Halpern, *Social Capital* (Polity, 2005), 38.

4. Alejandro Portes, "Social Capital: Its Origins and Applications in Modern Sociology," *Annual Review of Sociology*, (Vol. 24, 1998), 2.

5. Ibid., 19.

6. Halpern, op. cit., 210, 284, 13.

7. Ben Fine, *Social Capital Theory Versus Social Theory: Political Economy and Social Science at the Turn of the Millennium* (Routledge, 2001), 155.

8. Halpern, op. cit., 13.

9. Portes, op. cit., 2.

10. This is Marcella Ridlen Ray's paraphrasis of Mary Douglas' point in the former's *The Changing & Unchanging Face of U.S. Civil Society* (Transaction Publishers, 2002), 1.

11. Emile Durkheim, *The Division of Labor in Society* (Free Press, [1893] 1964), 28.

12. This is the phrase of Mustafa Emirbayer, Editor, *Emile Durkheim: Sociologist of Modernity* (Blackwell, 2003), 21.

13. This encapsulization of the Marxist model is provided by Randall Collins in *Theoretical Sociology* (Harcourt Brace Jovanovich, 1988), 90.

14. Max Weber, *The Protestant Ethic and the Spirit of Capitalism* (Scribner's, [1904-5] 1958).

15. Max Weber, "The Protestant Sects and the Spirit of Capitalism" in *From Max Weber: Essays in Sociology*, edited by Hans H. Gerth and C. Wright Mills (Oxford University Press, 1972), 311-312.

16. See Collins, op. cit. 152-153.

17. Emile Durkheim, *Suicide: A Study in Sociology* (Free Press, 1951), 386.

18. Peter L. Berger and Richard John Neuhaus, *To Empower People: From State to Civil Society* (American Enterprise Institute for Public Policy Research, 1977), 21.

19. This is addressed in the discussion of Halpern, op. cit., 224.

20. Nan Marie Astone, Constance A. Nathanson, Robert Schoen and Young J. Kim, "Family Demography, Social Theory, and Investment in Social Capital," *Population and Development Review* (March 1999), 6.

21. Ibid., 18.

22. Brian J. Jones, Bernard J. Gallagher III and Joseph A. McFalls, Jr., *Sociology: Micro, Macro, and Megastructures* (Harcourt Brace, 1995), 103.

23. Ibid., 109-113. This is not to imply that networks are universally beneficial. The negative side of networks is discussed on p. 113.

24. Nan Lin, *Social Capital: A Theory of Social Structure and Action* (Cambridge University Press, 2001), 25.

25. Putnam, op. cit., 91.

26. Putnam, op. cit., 407.

27. Halpern, op. cit., 53.

28. D. Cohen and L. Prusak, *In Good Company: How Social Capital Makes Organizations Work* (Free Press, 2001), 10.

29. Portes, op. cit., 13-15.

30. John Ehrenberg, *Civil Society: The Critical History of an Idea* (NYU Press, 1999), 248.

31. Astone, et. al., op. cit., 12. This point is also made by Portes, op. cit., 4.

32. Durkheim, *The Division of Labor in Society*, XXXIX.

33. Ibid., XXXVIII.

34. Multivariate analysis of variance (MANOVA, also referred to as n-way and multi-factor analysis of variance) was originally developed for experimental applications, but has been subsumed within the general linear model widely available in survey analysis packages such as the present version of MicroCase (see also Marija J. Norusis, "Balancing on Beams: Multivariate Analysis of Variance," *SPSS-X: Advanced Statistics Guide* (McGraw-Hill, 1985), 193-224). Like regression analysis, it is tested for significance using the F statistic for explained variance, but MANOVA offers three comparative advantages in the present application. First, it presents a much more flexible format for categorical independent variables. Instead of repeated dummy variable analyses in multiple regression, MANOVA incorporates categorical along with interval independent variables directly into the model. Second, as explained in text, MANOVA does not perform statistical controls by simply pulling out the variance explained by a given variable (like for partial correlation coefficients in multiple regression or MANOVA "covariates"); rather, the technique runs separate analyses *within* the categories of the control variable that can be compared visually and statistically. The third advantage is related to the second: MANOVA offers routine tests of multivariate interactions. If voluntary association has declined more for black than white Americans over time (true; see Chapter 9), that will automatically emerge as a two-variable interaction effect. There are tests for statistical interaction in multiple regression analysis as well, but the MANOVA format is much more direct and elegant than interpreting a series of dummy regression variables. Refer to Gudmund R. Iversen and Helmut Norpath, *Analysis of Variance* (Sage Publications, 1985).

35. Emile Durkheim, *Education and Sociology* (Free Press, 1956), 72.

36. Ibid., 244.

37. Halpern, op. cit., 233.

38. Putnam discusses the methodological matter of using statistical controls for education in Appendix I of *Bowling Alone*. He is acutely aware that education tends to raise social capital and that education itself has risen over this period. Given that, Putnam reasons "... the more *conservative* course is *not* to control for education," when arguing that social capital in America is in decline. This is true as far as it goes and is directly examined in Chapter 9 below, but of estimating his overall (downward) effects, Putnam

says the following: "*Virtually every generalization in this book has been subjected to detailed statistical analysis of this [multiple regression] sort, controlling simultaneously for age (or year of birth), gender,* EDUCATION, *income, race, marital status, parental status, job status (working full-time, part time, or not at all), and size at community of residence*" [emphasis added]. This practice would render many of my findings invisible. Entering education directly into the MANOVA model allows a direct view of what is happening for each level while retaining the technical rigor of regression-style models.

39. Glen C. Loury, "Why Should We Care about Group Inequality?" *Social Philosophy and Policy*, (1987: 5), 249-271.

40. Rodney Hero, *Racial Diversity and Social Capital: Equality and Community in America* (Cambridge University Press, 2007), 31.

41. Its general relevance is strongly suggested by Putnam's routine inclusion of gender as a control in his analyses described in Note #38 immediately above; Halpern offers a nice overview of age and social capital in op. cit., 248.

CHAPTER 3

1. Diane Fassel, *Working Ourselves to Death: The High Costs of Workaholism and the Rewards of Recovery* (Luniverse, 2000); Bryan E. Robinson, *Chained to the Desk: A Guide for Workaholics, Their Partners and Children, and the Clinicians Who Treat Them* (NYU Press, 1998); Paul Thorne and Michael Johnson, *Getting a Life in the Killing Fields of Work* (Diane, 2000).

2. Benjamin Franklin, "The Way to Wealth," at http://itech.fgcu.edu/faculty/ wohlpart/alra/ franklin.htm.

3. Juliet B. Schor, *The Overworked American: The Unexpected Decline of Leisure* (*Basic Books*, 1992), 28-29, 1-2. The substance of the trend in work hours and leisure in America is under some dispute in the professional literature. In *Time for Life: The Surprising Ways Americans Use Their Time* (Penn State University Press, 1997), John P. Robinson and Geoffrey Godbey use time-diary studies to dispute claims of a major change. For a moderating view, see Jerry A. Jacobs and Kathleen Gerson, "Who Are the Overworked Americans?" *Review of Social Economy* (Winter, 1998), 443-450.

4. Lawrence Mishel, Jared Bernstein and Heather Boushey, *The State of Working America 2002/2003* (ILR Press, 2003), 423.

5. Putnam, op. cit., 116.

6. Mishel, Bernstein and Boushey, op. cit. The labor force participation rates for the SCCBS reported here are remarkably similar to those of the Economic Policy Institute for the U.S.: males 71.8%, females 57.7% (p. 423).

Chi-square for Table 3.1 = 1690.7, p < .001.

7. The survey asked respondents to report their "average weekly work hours."

Chi-Square for Table 3.2 = 2009.0, p < .001.

8. Jones, op. cit., 530.

9. Chi-square for Table 3.3 = 5338.1, p < .001.

10. Chi-square for Table 3.4 = 1325.9, p < .001.

11. The 5% rule is conservative because in recent years the GSS moved the sample size up to n = 3,000, thus reducing sampling error even further. Chi-square values and probability levels are reported in the Notes (see immediately above and below), but of course the "specialists" referred to in-text will realize that the massive number of cases available in this cumulative data file make statistical significance very easy to achieve.

Chi-square for Table 3.5 = 126.2, p < .001.

12. The chi-square for Table 3.6a = 200.6, p < .001; for Table 3.6b = 661.4, p < .001; for Table 3.6c = 71.5, p < .001.

13. The chi-square for Table 3.7a = 212.0, p < .001; for Table 3.7b = 519.5, p < .001; for Table 3.7c = 71.5, p < .001.

14. The social network analyses overviewed in Chapter 2 focus on job *getting* via "networking," not on work effort *on* the job.

15. The chi-square for Table 3.8a = 23.7, p = .008; for Table 3.8b = 224.5, p < .001; for Table 3.8c = 118.3, p < .001.

CHAPTER 4

1. Astone, et al., op. cit., 18.

2. For Table 4.1, chi-square = 643.2, p < .001.

3. For Table 4.2, chi-square = 1704.0, p < .001.

4. For Table 4.3, chi-square = 716.5, p < .001.

5. For Table 4.4, chi-square = 1370.0, p < .001.

6. For Table 4.5a, chi-square = 365.5, p < .001. For Table 4.5b, chi-square = 535.0, p < .001.

7. For Table 4.6a, chi-square = 379.9, p < .001. For Table 4.6b, chi-square = 687.9, p < .001. For Table 4.6c, chi-square = 278.8, p < .001.

8. For Table 4.7a, chi-square = 409.7, p < .001. For Table 4.7b, chi-square = 652.2, p < .001. For Table 4.7c, chi-square = 124.8, p < .001.

9. Citation of Urie Bronfenbrenner, Statement at Hearings before the Committee on Ways and Means, House of Representatives, 91st Congress (U.S. Govt. Printing Office, 1969, 1837-1838), in Urie Bronfenbrenner, Peter McClelland, Elaine Wethington, Phyllis Moen, and Stephen J. Ceci, *The State of Americans: This Generation and the Next* (The Free Press, 1996), viii.

10. For documentation of the stabilization in the divorce rate based on numerous data sources including the U.S. Census, refer to Jay D. Teachman, Lucky M. Tedrow and Kyle D. Crowder, "The Changing Demography of America's Families," *Journal of Marriage and the Family* (November 2000), 1234-1246.

11. Tom W. Smith, "Ties that Bind: The Emerging 21st Century Family," *Public Perspective* (January/February 2001), 34.

12. Mary Ann Mason, Arlene Skolnick and Stephen D. Sugarman, *All Our Families: New Policies for a New Century* (Oxford University Press, 1998), 20.

13. For an overview of such surveys, see David Popenoe and Barbara Dafoe Whitehead, "The State of Our Unions 2000: The Social Health of Marriage in America," The National Marriage Project, at http://marriage.rutgers.edu/state_of_our_unions %202000%20text%20only.htm.

CHAPTER 5

1. Putnam, op. cit. The six chapters constituting the "So What" section of the book offer a plenitude of evidence on the effects of social networks.

2. World Values Survey, 1995-1997. www.worldvaluessurvey.org.

Actually, three other societies were slightly above the U.S.A. on this item atop the list of countries, but the top four were all between 69.4% and 71.6%.

3. Chi-square for Table 5.1 = 89.3, p < .001.

4. Chi-square for Table 5.2 = 198.9, p < .001.

5. Chi-square for Table 5.3 = 10.9, p = .012. This statistically significant result demonstrates the n-sensitivity of the chi-square statistic even with small substantive differences, and the consequent wisdom of sticking with the 5% difference standard.

6. Chi-square for Table 5.4 = 344.1, p < .001.

7. Chi-square for Table 5.5 = 71.4, p < .001.

8. Chi-square for Table 5.6 = 683.8, p < .001.

9. Chi-square for Table 5.7 = 528.6, p < .001.

10. Chi-square for Table 5.8 = 340.3, p < .001.

11. Chi-square for Table 5.9 = 393.9, p < .001.

12. Chi-square for Table 5.10 = 930.1, p < .001.

13. Chi-square for Table 5.11 = 77.8, p < .001.

14. Chi-square for Table 5.12 = 291.3, p < .001.

15. See Putnam, op. cit., 23-24.

16. Chi-square for Table 5.13a = 7.5, p = .113 (not significant); for Table 5.13b = 23.7, p = .001.

17. Chi-square for Table 5.14a = 24.3, p < .001; for Table 5.14b = 8.2, p < .001.

18. Chi-square for Table 5.15a = 39.9, p < .001; for Table 5.15b = 81.6, p < .001.

19. Chi-square for Table 5.16a = 16.9, p = .002; for Table 5.16b = 17.6, p = .001; for Table 5.16c = 23.6, p < .001.

20. Chi-square for Table 5.17a = 7.4, p = .118 (not significant); for Table 5.17b = 2.2, p = .700 (not significant); for Table 5.17c = 11.5, p = .021.

21. Chi-square for Table 5.18a = 36.5, p < .001; for Table 5.18b = 44.3, p < .001; for Table 5.18c = 24.8, p < .001.

22. Chi-square for Table 5.19a = 16.9, p = .002; for Table 5.19b = 4.1, p = .389 (not significant); for Table 5.19c = 4.4, p = .357 (not significant).

23. Chi-square for Table 5.20a = 20.4, p < .001 (there is a 6.1% surge in the 80s, which subsides to under 5% in the 90s); for Table 5.20b = 1.0, p = .912 (not significant); for Table 5.20c = 5.4, p = .246 (not significant).

24. Chi-square for Table 5.21a = 12.7, p = .012; for Table 5.21b = 59.3, p < .001; for Table 5.21c = 40.5, p < .001.

CHAPTER 6

1. For an excellent overview of the empirical studies refer to James E. Curtis, Douglas E. Baer and Edward G. Grabb, "Nations of Joiners: Explaining Voluntary Association Membership in Democratic Societies," *American Sociological Review* (December, 2001), 783-806. Their own analyses find the United States to be slightly behind the Nordic societies in levels of membership, but still near the top with about twice the average of the other 32 societies in the sample.

2. For Table 6.1, chi-square = 68.1, p < .001.

3. John Wilson and Marc Musick, "Who Cares? Toward an Integrated Theory of Volunteer Work," *American Sociological Review* (62, 1997), 694-713.

4. Susan Eckstein, "Community as Gift-Giving: Collectivistic Roots of Volunteerism," *American Sociological Review* (December, 2001), 829.

5. John Wilson, "Volunteering," *Annual Review of Sociology* (26, 2000), 215-240.

6. See Putnam, op. cit., 128.

7. For Table 6.2, chi-square = 163.4, p < .001. This finding is in accord with the gender generalization in Wilson's literature review, op. cit., 237.

8. For Table 6.3, chi-square = 341.5, p < .001.

9. Putnam, op. cit., 249.

10. Putnam, op. cit., 127-128.

11. Again from Wilson's literature review, "Since data gathering on volunteering from national samples began about a quarter of a century ago, the rate for the U.S. has been stable or, according to some studies, rising slightly." Op. cit., 215.

12. Wilson, op. cit., 226. For Table 6.4, chi-square = 212.4, p < .001.

13. Putnam, op. cit., 18.

14. Wilson, op. cit., 220.

15. For Table 6.5, chi-square = 2855.1, p < .001.

16. For Table 6.6, chi-square = 1865.2, p < .001.

17. For Table 6.7, chi-square = 68.4, p < .001. For Table 6.8, chi-square = 111.1, p < .001.

18. These Voluntary Association II items were administered fifteen times over the relevant period: four times each in the 1970s and 1990s, and seven times during the 1980s.

19. Recall that the SCCBS survey included eighteen types of groups compared to these sixteen from the GSS.

20. For Table 6.9a, chi-square = 16.0, p = .003. For Table 6.9b, chi-square = 20.9, p < .001. Again, the prodigious cumulative sample sizes are inflating chi-square values.

21. Putnam, op. cit., 278.

22. For Table 6.10a, chi-square = 26.7, p < .001. For Table 6.10b, chi-square = 20.0, p < .001.

23. For Table 6.11a, chi-square = 5.9, p = .205 (not significant). For Table 6.11b, chi-square = 14.6, p=.005. Even with the usual caution about inflated sample size, it should be noted that the latter subtable shows movement in an upward direction.

24. For Table 6.12a, chi-square = 6.1, p = .191 (not significant). For Table 6.12b, chi-square = 28.0, p < .001. For Table 6.12c, chi-square = 4.6, p = .330 (not significant).

25. For Table 6.13a, chi-square = 2.5, p = .649 (not significant). For Table 6.13b, chi-square = 59.5, p < .001. For Table 6.13c, chi-square = 10.0, p = .040.

For Table 6.14a, chi-square = 0.8, p = .938 (not significant). For Table 6.14b, chi-square = 3.6, p = .460 (not significant). For Table 6.14c, chi-square = 3.9, p = .416 (not significant).

26. For Table 6.15a, chi-square = 28.2, p < .001. For Table 6.15b, chi-square = 41.9, p < .001. For Table 6.15c, chi-square = 3.4, p = .499 (not significant).

27. For Table 6.16a, chi-square = 29.4, p < .001. For Table 6.16b, chi-square = 48.6, p < .001. for Table 6.16c, chi-square = 19.4, p < .001.

28. For Table 6.17a, chi-square = 10.6, p = .031. For Table 6.17b, chi-square = 16.7, p = .002. For Table 6.17c, chi-square = 8.2, p = .085.

CHAPTER 7

1. Hazel Morris, "Satellites Hunt for Buried Treasure," *New Scientist*, July 10, 2003.

2. The technique's special statistical advantages in the present application are introduced and explained in Chapter 2. See especially Note #34.

3. The hourly averages are 35.8 to 18.4, respectively.

4. The hourly averages are 26.2 to 12.9, respectively.

5. The three-way interaction F = 16.5, p < .001

6. The three-way interaction F = 22.3, p < .001.

7. For an excellent overview, see Miller McPherson, Lynn Smith-Lovin and James M. Cook, "Birds of a Feather: Homophily in Social Networks," *Annual Review of Sociology* (27:1), 415-444.

8. This variable is an index of items from the SCCBS including the frequency of having friends visit one's home, visiting with relatives, socializing with co-workers outside of work, hanging out with friends in public places, and playing cards and board games.

9. For the MANOVA main effect, $F = 261.3$, $p < .001$. Education level is utilized here as a covariate.

10. For the main effect, $F = 335.5$, $p < .001$.

11. 3.4 to 2.4 memberships, respectively.

12. These three variables were statistically controlled as covariates.

13. More precisely, the across the board average for Americans in the SCCBS is 2.964. For the MANOVA main effect, $F = 67.3$, $p < .001$.

14. For the MANOVA main effect, $F = 40.5$, $p < .001$.

15. For the MANOVA main effect, $F = 56.0$, $p < .001$.

16. The available responses for the item were, $0 =$ none, $1 =$ one or two, $2 =$ three to five, $3 =$ six to ten, $4 =$ over ten.

For the MANOVA main effect, $F = 11.1$, $p < .001$.

17. For the gender-work hours interaction effect, $F = 2.5$, $p = 0.026$.

18. For the age-work hours interaction effect, $F = 11.8$, $p < .001$.

19. The actual average is 16.793. For the MANOVA main effect, $F = 49.6$, $p < .001$.

20. For the MANOVA main effect, $F = 33.5$, $p < .001$. The .2 difference is actually somewhat compressed because the friend numbers have been grouped into categories (e.g., "six to ten").

21. Unmarried with no children respondents average 21.424 visits per year compared to 24.946 for those married with children. For the MANOVA main effect, $F = 52.4$, $p < .001$.

22. For the MANOVA main effect, $F = 119.9$, $p < .001$.

23. For the family structure-age interaction effect, $F = 77.2$, $p < .001$.

24. For the family structure-age interaction effect, $F = 9.2$, $p < .001$.

25. Over this age span, married with children respondents increase from 2.366 to 4.164 groups; neither of the other family status increases their average by even 1 group. For the family structure-age interaction effect, $F = 14.1$, $p < .001$.

Chapter 8

1. Unless otherwise noted, age (as an interval variable), education level (by degree to parallel the coding in the SCCBS) and sex will be entered as covariates. For the three-way interaction effect, $F = 9.5$, $p < .001$.

2. For the main effect for voluntary association, $F = 52.3$, $p < .001$. The two-way test for an interaction with decade was not statistically significant ($F = 1.3$, $p = .213$).

3. The test for the two-way interaction of decade and work hours was not statistically significant ($F = 1.4$, $p = .168$).

4. For the three-way interaction effect, $F = 1.9$, $p = 0.039$. The interpretation is that the work hours-nonyouth group relationship has changed over time, but especially so for males.

5. It is interesting to note that membership in "sports groups" has risen significantly among part-timer males. A resurgence of bowling teams, perhaps?

6. For the MANOVA main effect for decade, $F = 7.7$, $p < .001$. The test for the two-way interaction of decade and work hours was not statistically significant ($F = 1.5$, $p = .141$).

7. For the two-way interaction of sex and decade, $F = 4.6$, $p = .010$.

8. For the MANOVA main effect for decade, $F = 30.3$, $p < .001$. None of the interaction effects with age were statistically significant.

9. For the MANOVA main effect for decade, $F = 5.5$, $p = .004$. For the main effect of family structure, $F = 310.9$, $p < .001$.

10. For the MANOVA main effect for decade, $F = 6.2$, $p = .002$. For the main effect of family structure, $F = 33.5$, $p < .001$.

11. For the MANOVA main effect for decade, $F = 69.0$, $p < .001$. For the main effect of family structure, $F = 112.8$, $p < .001$.

12. For the three-way interaction of decade-family structure-age representing this "shift," $F = 3.0$, $p = .003$. This F-value is less than one-fifth the size of the two-variable interaction representing the consistent family structure-age effect (see below).

13. For the two-way family structure-age interaction, $F = 16.0$, $p < .001$.

14. See especially Putnam, op. cit., Chapter 14.

CHAPTER 9

1. Tocqueville, op. cit., 9.

2. Ehrenberg, op. cit., 61.

3. Putnam, op. cit. (2007), 156.

4. Ehrenberg, op. cit., 61.

5. For an overview of both trends, refer to Orlando Patterson, *The Ordeal of Integration* (Civitas, 1997).

6. The phrase and support for using education as a proxy for social class is from Robert Perrucci and Earl Wysong, *The New Class Society: Goodbye American Dream?* (Rowman & Littlefield, 2008), 260.

7. For the two-way education level-decade interaction effect, $F = 5.5$, $p < .001$.

8. For the two-way education level-decade interaction effect, $F = 9.0$, $p < .001$.

9. For the three-way education level-decade-race interaction effect, $F = 3.0$, $p = .016$.

10. The overall means vary between 1.739 and 1.820 groups, but as the Figure shows they move slightly down then up across the decades.

11. For the MANOVA main effect of decade, $F = 19.3$, $p < .001$.

12. For the race-decade interaction effect, $F = 3.2$, $p = .042$.

13. In simple crosstabulations, the decline in membership in these two groups is approximately 8% for black Americans compared to 5% for white Americans.

14. See Bruce Western, *Between Class and Market: Postwar Unionization in the Capitalist Democracies* (Princeton University Press, 1997).

15. That trend was forecast by the classical sociological thinkers cited in Chapter 2: Emile Durkheim, Karl Marx and Max Weber. There is a contemporary debate on whether the secularization thesis should be discarded or altered. For an excellent discussion of both sides in this debate, see Ronald Inglehart and Pippa Norris, *Sacred and Secular: Religion and Politics Worldwide* (Cambridge University Press, 2004).

16. This precise point about exogenous causes of the decline of these two types of groups is made by Carl Boggs, "Social Capital and Political Fantasy," *Theory and Society* (Vol. 30, 2001), 284.

17. Refer to James P. Smith and Finis R. Welch, "Black Economic Progress after Myrdal," *Journal of Economic Literature* (June 1989), 519-564. See also June O'Neill, "The Role of Human Capital in Earnings Differences Between Black and White Men," *The Journal of Economic Perspectives* (Fall 1990), 25-45.

18. For the two-way race-education level interaction effect, $F = 8.8$, $p < .001$.

19. For the two-way race-education level interaction effect, $F = 7.5$, $p < .001$.

20. For the two-way race-education level interaction effect, $F = 6.9$, $p = .001$.

21. For the two-way race-education level interaction effect, $F = 4.7$, $p = .009$. By comparison, the main effect of education is $F = 966.7$, $p < .001$.

22. Grace Kao, "Social Capital and Its Relevance to Minority and Immigrant Populations," *Sociology of Education* (Vol. 77), 175.

CHAPTER 10

1. Barry Glassner, *The Culture of Fear: Why Americans are Afraid of the Wrong Things* (Basic Books, 1999), 60-61.

2. Barry Glassner, Ibid., 60.

3. Katherine S. Newman, op. cit., *Rampage: The Social Roots of School Shootings* (Basic Books, 2004), ix.

4. Katherine S. Newman, Ibid., 51-54.

5. Brian J. Jones, Joseph A. McFalls Jr. and Bernard J. Gallagher III, "Toward a Unified Model for Social Problems Theory," *Journal for the Theory of Social Behavior* (Sept. 1989, Vol. 19), 337-356.

6. Katherine S. Newman, op. cit., 49.

7. Katherine S. Newman, op. cit., 111-112.

8. Katherine S. Newman, op. cit., 125; 111-112.

9. Robert Putnam, op. cit., 216.

10. Robert Putnam, op. cit., 43.

11. For the MANOVA main effect of TV hours, $F = 74.2$, $p < .001$. By comparison, for the education level main effect, $F = 1012.4$, $p < .001$.

12. For the MANOVA main effect of TV hours, $F = 7.6$, $p = .001$. By comparison, for the education level main effect, $F = 112.1$, $p < .001$. There is also a two-way education level-TV hours interaction effect ($F = 2.8$, $p = 0.025$), which is indicated by somewhat more variation among the less than high school respondents (note the perceptible up, then down movement in the Figure).

13. According to the MANOVA mean estimates, college respondents watch about an hour a day less than high school respondents, and approaching two hours a day less than less than high school respondents.

14. The actual averages are 3.388 groups for 0-1 TV hours and 2.465 groups for 4+ hours.

For the MANOVA main effect of work hours, $F = 82.6$, $p < .001$; by comparison, for the main effect of TV hours, $F = 61.1$, $p < .001$.

15. For the MANOVA main effect for family structure, $F = 71.3$, $p < .001$; for TV hours, $F = 59.6$, $p < .001$. The two-way interaction effect for family structure-TV hours is $F = 2.4$, $p = .045$.

16. In *Bowling Alone*, Putnam presents evidence for changes in the civic life of remote Canadian towns recently introduced to television, but he is quite clear on the point that there is no decisive evidence on the direction of causation. See op. cit., 235-237.

17. The overall averages are 1970s = 2.921, 1980s = 3.009 and 1990s = 2.906.

18. For the two-way race-TV hours interaction effect, $F = 4.5$, $p = .011$.

19. Putnam, op. cit. 179.

20. For the MANOVA main effect for WWW hours, $F = 170.8$, $p < .001$. For the two-way WWW hours-education level interaction effect, $F = 5.2$, $p < .001$.

The group averages go from 1.458 at no internet time to 2.722 at 6+ hours for less than high school respondents; for college respondents the averages are 3.330 to 3.885, respectively.

21. For the MANOVA main effect for WWW hours, $F = 54.6$, $p < .001$. For the two-way WWW hours-education level interaction effect , $F = 9.5$, $p < .001$.

22. For the MANOVA main effect for WWW hours in Figure 10.7a, $F = 158.0$, $p < .001$.

23. For the MANOVA main effect for WWW hours in Figure 10.7b, $F = 166.8$, $p < .001$.

About the Author

Brian Jones is Professor of Sociology at Villanova University. He has written extensively on issues in public policy and social networks, and his previous books include *Social Problems: Issues, Opinions, and Solutions* and *Sociology: Micro, Macro, and Megastructures.* Dr. Jones is a lifelong Philadelphia area resident who received his B.A., M.A. and Ph.D. degrees at the University of Pennsylvania